MORE

MORE

BY

MAX BEERBOHM

FOURTH EDITION

Essay Index Reprint Series

BOOKS FOR LIBRARIES PRESS, INC.
FREEPORT, NEW YORK

FOURTH EDITION First Published 1921
Reprinted 1967

LIBRARY OF CONGRESS CATALOG CARD NUMBER:
67-28730

PRINTED IN THE UNITED STATES OF AMERICA

TO

MLLE. DE LA RAMÉE

WITH THE AUTHOR'S COMPLIMENTS

AND TO

OUIDA

WITH HIS LOVE

From inilluminable catacombs — *to wit, files of the* Saturday Review, *the* Daily Mail, *the* Outlook, Tomorrow, *and the* Musician, *to whose editors I am indebted for much courtesy* — *I have rescued these few creatures of my fancy, deeming them perhaps worthy of a brighter haven. There was a host of others, which Sentiment urged me to rescue also. But I have forborne. Nor have I admitted to this haven any of these little creatures without scrutiny and titivation.*

M. B.

CONTENTS

SOME WORDS ON ROYALTY

In the memoirs of Count *, privately printed last year, you will find, if you can gain access to them, many secrets told in a sprightly, yet most authoritative, manner ; little that is incredible, little that is not amazing, nothing refutable. The Count has cast upon *la haute politique*, that stage without footlights, many lurid "limes," illuminating for us the faces of all the players and even enabling us to understand something of the plot. For years the trusted Minister of the late Emperor § of †, the Count has much court-lore to communicate, and is terribly frank about the master whom he served so faithfully until, in 188‡, he was ousted from favour by the machinations of a jealous and not too scrupulous cabal. I, who had always been taught to regard this monarch as a wise, gifted, and courageous gentleman, if not actually as a hero, am pleasantly shocked to find him designated

with such unkind terms as "*fainéant*," — the memoirs
are written in the Volapuk of diplomacy — and "*roi de
paille*," and "*petit bonhomme à tête montée.*" Indeed,
it is undoubtedly when he is describing the life and the
character of the Emperor that my author is at his most
intimate, his best. Seldom has so realistic a portrait of
a modern monarch been painted for our pleasure. Much
as we talk and read about royal personages, we know
really less about them than about any other kind of
human beings. We see the princes of our country cara-
coling past us in pageants, illustrious monsters whose
breasts are all agleam and aglimmer with the symbols of
fifty victories at which they were not present, and bunt
with enough ribandry to trick forth fifty dairymaids for a
fair. We tell ourselves that beneath all their frippery
they are human beings. We have heard that one is
industrious, another is genial, another plays the fiddle or
collects stamps. And then, maybe, we see them at
Newmarket, and we know that, for all the elaborate
simplicity of their tweeds and billycocks, they are not as
we are, but, rather, creatures of another order, " specimens of an unrelated species." We note the curious
uniformity of their faces, almost wondering whether they
are masked. Those heavy, handsome, amiable, uninter-

4

esting and uninterested faces, are they indeed (not masks but) true mirrors of souls which a remote and esoteric life has gradually impoverished ? We know that there is a crimson drugget which underlies their every footstep from the cradle to the mausoleum ; we know that their progress is beneath an awning, along that level drugget, through an unbroken avenue of bare and bowed heads. They cannot mingle with their fellows. They are kept from all contact with realities. For them there is no reciprocity, no endeavour, no salt of life. " It is a miserable State of Minde," wrote a philosopher who was also a courtier, " to have few Things to desire and many Things to feare. And yet that commonly is the case of Princes." Fear kept human the Princes of other days. We have taken away their fear now, and we still leave them no loophole for desire. What, we might well wonder, will be the descendants of this race apart, of these men who neither marry nor give in marriage save among their own order ? Would any one choose to be born, in their purple, to their life of morbid and gaudy humdrum ? Better, surely, to be thrown, like the ordinary child, into a life of endeavour, with unforeseen chances of success or failure. It is this scroll of chances that makes life tolerable, makes it wonderful. The life

5

of every royal person in England begins and must needs
end on the same high, smooth plane. But who shall
cast the horoscope of an ordinary child? Who knows
the vicissitudes of his journey? Be he suckled in a pit,
or in a castle on a mountain, who shall prophesy the level
of his last bed? Cast him up naked to the pit's edge,
send him in purple down the wide steps of his father's
castle, you know not how long he shall fare in the gloom
or light of his origin, nor whither, and by what hostel-
ries, he shall pass. He may come to a dark woodland,
where, all night long, the ferns snap under the feet of
elusive Dryads, and the moon is privy to the whole grief
of Philomel. He may never leave that gentle labyrinth
of leaves, or he may tarry there but for one night.
Mocked and footsore, he may shuffle along the highways,
till he come to that city whose people stone him or make
him ruler over them. Exile or empery may be his,
flowers or ashes, an aureole or a noose. There are seas
for his drowning, and whirlwinds for his overwhelming,
and sheer rocks for his ascent. He shall clutch and falter
and be afraid. No bloodhounds but shall follow swiftly
on his track, nor any nets but shall enmesh him. He
shall laugh and conquer. He shall prosper in a great
dominion. In strength and scorn there shall not be his

6

equal. But the slaves whom he tortured shall prick him in his exultation. His wine-cup shall be a cup of gall, and a harpy shall lurk in the canopy of his bridal bed. In the blood of his children they shall bathe him. From a clear sky the lightning shall slant down on him. And the ground shall yawn for him in the garden of his design.

That, despite certain faults of exaggeration, is a piece of quite admirable prose; but let it not decoy the reader from consideration of the main theme. Count *, whose memoirs are my cue, does not seem to have weighed the conditions of royal life. Had he done so, he would have cooled his caustic pen in the lymph of charity, and one would have lost many of his most delightful *mots* and anecdotes. He simply records, out of the fulness and intimacy of his knowledge, many suggestive facts about a monarch in whom a royal environment had not paralysed the ordinary, bright instincts of human nature. In recording with gusto the little strategies used by his master in the pursuit of fun or the flight from duty, the Count moves his reader to tears rather than to laughter.

One of his anecdotes I must really make known, not merely because it is a good sample and deals with a famous incident, but also because it has a suggestive sym-

7

bolism of its own. Many of my readers can remember the sensation caused in the spring of a late seventy by the attempted assassination of Emperor §. As his Imperial Majesty was being driven out of the palace gates for his daily progress through the capital, a man in the crowd fired at him with a revolver. The miscreant was immediately seized, and, but for the soldiery, would have been torn limb from limb. "Luckily," wrote Reuter's correspondent, "the Emperor, who was accompanied as usual by Count" * "and an aide-de-camp, was untouched. As so often happens in such cases, the assassin, doubtless through excitement, entirely missed his aim. The remarkable thing was the coolness and courage displayed by the Emperor. So far from evincing any alarm, he continued to salute the crowd on either side, smilingly as ever, as though nothing at all had happened; nor was his drive in any way curtailed. As the news spread, a vast crowd of people collected round the palace, and the Emperor, in answer to their continued cheers, at length appeared upon the balcony and bowed repeatedly."

In the light of the Count's version the Emperor's "coolness and courage" are somewhat discounted. It seems that, about three years before, the Emperor had

8

declared that he was going to give up the custom of the daily drive : he hated driving, he hated saluting, he hated being stared at. The Count represented to him how unwise it would be to disappoint the people. Finding the Emperor obstinate in his distaste, he conceived the idea of a waxen figure, made in the likeness of his master, with practicable joints worked by interior mechanism. The Emperor promised to endure his drives for the present, and, after secret negotiations with a famous firm in England (conducted by the Count himself, who came over incognito), the figure was completed and duly delivered at the Imperial Palace. It was so constructed that, when wound up, it turned its head slowly from side to side, with a slight bend of the body, raising its hand in salute. It was considered an admirable likeness, though the Count declares that " *la figure était un peu trop distinguée.*" At any rate, arrayed as a Colonel of the || Dragoons and driven quickly through the capital, it was good enough to deceive the Emperor's loyal subjects. As I need hardly say, it was at this automaton that the revolver was fired. According to the memoirs, the Emperor himself, in a false beard, was standing near the assassin, and was actually arrested on suspicion, but managed to escape his captor in the *mêlée* and reached the

9

palace in ample time to bow from the balcony. The Count argues that the only sufferer in the affair is the poor wretch who was hanged merely for shooting at a dummy, and who has never even got the credit he deserved for a very good shot; the bullet pierced right through the dummy's chest, and, says the Count, had it but lodged one-eighth of an inch lower down, it must have inevitably stopped the mechanism.

Even if the whole of this tale be but the naughty figment of a favourite in disfavour, it is, at any rate, suggestive. A mob doffing its headgear, day after day, to a dummy! How easily, after all, could one get a dummy so constructed as to hold a *levée* or sit through an opera, to open a bridge or lay a stone " well and truly." There are some persons who would fain abolish altogether the institution of royalty. I do not go far as they. Our royal family is a rather absurd institution, no doubt. But then, humanity itself is rather absurd. A State can never be more than a kindergarten, at best, and he who would fain rule men according to principles of right reason will fare no better than did poor dear Plato at Syracuse. Put the dream of the *doctrinaire* into practice, and it will soon turn to some such nightmare as modern France or modern America. Indeed, fallacies and anomalies are the basis of all good government. A Crown, like a Garter, implies no " damned merit : " else were it void of its impressive magic for most creatures. Strictly, there is no reason why we should worship the House of Hanover more than we worship any other family. Strictly, there was no reason why the Children of Israel should bow down before brazen images. But man is not rational, and the spirit of idolatry is strong in him. And, if you take away his idol, that energy which would otherwise be spent in kotowing will probably be spent in some less harmless manner. In every free public there is a fund of patriotic emotion which must, somehow, be worked off. I may be insular, but I cannot help thinking it better that this fund should be worked off, as in England, by cheering the members of the royal family, rather than by upsetting the current ministry, as in France.

The main good of royalty, then, and the justification of those fabulous sums of money that we sacrifice annually for its support, lie in its appeal to that idolatrous instinct which is quite unmoved by the cheap and nasty inmates of the Elysée or of the White House. In this century we have greatly restricted the sphere of royal power, insomuch that royalty cannot, as it once could, guide directly the tend of politics : politically, it does but " act by its presence.'' But one should not forget that a Court is for ornament, as well as for use. A capital without a Court, be the streets never so beautiful, is even as a garden where the sun shines not. As a flock of sheep without a shepherd, so is the Society that has no royal leader to set its fashions, chasten its follies, or dignify its whims with his approval. Gaiety, wit, beauty, some measure even of splendour, may be compassed in the *salons* of a republic; but distinction comes not in save with one who must be received at the foot of the staircase. In fact, royalty is indispensable : we cannot spare it. But, you may well ask, are we justified in preserving an institution which ruins the lives and saps the human nature of a whole family ? What of those royal victims whom we sacrifice to our expediency ? I have suggested that royal functions could be quite satisfactorily performed by automata made of wax. There, I think, lies the solution of our difficulty. Perhaps, even now, did we but know, it is the triumphs of Tussaud at whose frequent sight our pulses beat with so quick an enthusiasm. If it is so, I do not blame our royal family for its innocent subterfuge. I should welcome any device to lighten the yoke that is on their necks. I should be glad if more people would seriously examine the conditions of royalty, with a view to ameliorating the royal lot. Would that every one could gain access to the memoirs of Count *! They might serve as an excellent manual, containing, as they do, so much that is well-observed. But they are so frankly written that they cannot, I fear, be made public before many, many years have elapsed. Perhaps the brief trumpet-note which I have sounded will be enough to rouse humanitarianism, in the meantime.

"PUNCH"

It is from the bound volumes of *Punch* that small boys derive their knowledge of life. That, I suppose, is why small boys are always so old-fashioned in their ideas. They do not — how should they? — know that lineal art can represent life and life's types only through certain symbols, certain conventions: they imagine these symbols and conventions to be realistic portraiture. Even in later years, when they have detected how wide and fluid a thing life is, they do yet conceive many real things through the false conventions of John Tenniel, George Du Maurier, Charles Keene, and the rest. I myself, steeped in Du Maurier's innumerable drawings, am always surprised when I see a *nouveau riche* whose shirtfront no diamond stud irradiates with conventional lines. Also, when I go to a party of any kind, I expect always to find there, grouped impressively,

an elderly Statesman with a star and riband, a tall Artist
with a beard, a Bishop with gaiters, a long-haired Musician with a fiddle under his arm, an old General with a
grey moustache, and a young barrister with side-whiskers.
My study of Keene, likewise, has brought me to this
belief — in which I shall most likely die — that a tipsy
man always has a white cravat straggling over his left
shoulder, and that cabmen are, as a class, witty. But if
these two artists deceive me, dealing, so far as they
could, directly with life, how much more did Tenniel,
the maker of symbolic cartoons, deceive me ! *Beatus
insipiens*, I never dreamt that the Duke of Argyll did
not always wear a kilt. Even now, when I go to
France, I expect to see every man with moustache and
imperial, after the pattern of Louis Napoleon, and every
woman with short skirts, *sabots*, and cap-of-liberty. I
am not rid, even now, of the notion that every English
burglar goes about his work in knee-breeches, with a fur
cap on his head, a mask over his face, and a "jemmy"
protruding from a side-pocket. And so, whenever, in
the dead of night, I hear scrapings and shufflings down
below, I seek refuge in renewed sleep. Could I per-
suade myself that the burglar was but an ordinary individual in trousers, I would take candle and poker and send

18

him about his business. As it is, I am quite unable to
cope with burglars, and so they come rather often.
Thus may a man suffer for his ideals.

It is a painful thing, youth's awakening to the fallacies
of its first mentor, *Punch*. I remember well a great
shock I received in my first term at Oxford. I had
arranged to go with some other undergraduates to Kempton Park. I had never been on a race-course in my
life : my knowledge of race-courses was bounded by
Tenniel's annual cartoon for Derby Day, doubly impressive by reason of its double page. How horrified I
was, on the eve of the races, to hear that we were not
going to drive to Kempton on a coach ! " How else
could one go ? " I asked. " By train," my friends
answered. " But *can* one go to a race by train ? " I
objected ; " has it ever been done ? " My friends,
older and of more experience than I, assured me that
it was the only possible way. They assured me, the
next morning, when I joined their breakfast at the
" Mitre," that I could not possibly go " dressed like
that." (I was wearing a light frock-suit and a white
top-hat with a green veil round it. In my hand was an
open betting-book, and between my lips a small straw.)
I, in my turn, commented sarcastically upon their own

appearance. I told them that they might choose to make themselves ridiculous, but that I did not; that I should go alone to the races. Gradually they proved to me that I was in the wrong. I had just time to go back to my rooms, change my clothes, and catch the train. But I felt that the whole spirit of the thing had evaporated. When we reached the course, there was not one gipsy to tell me my fortune, nor any troupe of niggers to sing to me, nor any welsher for me to chase out of the ring and duck in a horse-pond. There was but a crowd of noisy and unremarkable persons, such as one might see any day in the Strand. No one snatched at my watch-chain. No dog ran down the cleared course, but only some outspread horses, which looked, in the distance, absurdly like the horses in that "race-game" of my childhood. My friends and I disbursed small sums of money to various book-makers, receiving small paper tickets in return. My friends and I gained nothing by our indiscriminate charity. The sun was ferociously hot. We left before the last race, dusty and reserved.

Well! As historian, *Punch* still holds his sway over little boys. But as jester for adults he is at present labouring under a cloud, and his weekly appearance is not

the event it yet was even within my recollection. No
one is excited nowadays at the prospect of *Punch ;* yet I
assure all my juniors that, when I was a small boy,
Wednesday morning marked an epoch in each week. So
early as Monday, the members of each family would
begin to revel in anticipation. Tuesday evening was
a time of ill-suppressed excitement, and, at bed-time,
sleep wooed even the eldest as coyly as it woos children
on their birthday-eves. When the sun rose, the most
incorrigible lie-a-bed could scarce await the delivery of
hot water. Even the cockscomb would telescope his
toilet. Family-prayers would be read quickly, sometimes even abbreviated for the day, and the last Amen
was ever signal for an ugly rush to the plate where the
new *Punch* was reposing. A bundle of heads, young
and old, hung over the crisp pages. What sort of
Britannia had Tenniel done ? How had Du Maurier
satirised Sir Gorgius Midas or Mrs. Ponsonby de
Tomkyns ? Had Sambourne made Gladstone into a
shark or a canary or a buffalo or what ? Not until night-
fall had the full sweets of the comic paper been exhausted.
Thursday was felt to be something of a blank, an anti-
climax.

But Time is a sad iconoclast, and this family idol,

though it has not been utterly shattered, has been knocked from its high pedestal. *Punch* still plays his part in English family home life, but his part is comparatively humble, and he no longer takes precedence of the morning paper. In the smoking-rooms of clubs, he contends with a score of comic rivals. Everybody affects to despise him, and his jokes merely raise the eyebrows of the community. " Don't you think that *Punch* gets more stupid every week ? " has superseded " Have you been to many theatres lately ? " Mr. Burnand has this consolation, at least, that his paper is not ignored. There are few people who do not look through it every week, and few who do not talk about it. Quite lately, indeed, it was the object of many attacks from other newspapers. One journal published, week by week, an unkind analysis of the current number. This " Scheme for the Reformation of *Punch* " was a thing of great unconscious humour — imagine a man sitting down, industriously marking the jokes which do not come up to his standard of wit, industriously copying them out, writing an article to explain their defects, and warning their makers that they must do better next week. Without wishing to perpetuate the use of an old and generally foolish sneer, I must say that such a proceeding was peculiarly English.

22

The *Star's* portentous *employé* did not stop short at criticism, but even dabbled in creation, apparently that we might see what humour can and should be. After eulogising Mr. Phil May, and expressing his regret that this artist had no worthy colleague on the staff, " *let us,*" he said brightly, " *have not only a Phil May, but also a Phil June, a Phil July, a Phil August, a Phil September, a Phil October, a Phil November, and a Phil December.*" It would be interesting to see the man who wrote that. But I do not agree with the writer's contempt for all Mr. May's colleagues. So far as I can see, the drawings in *Punch*, and the jokes they illustrate, are not less good than they have been in former times. Certainly they are better than the efforts of other comic papers. *Punch* is no longer the close concern it was when Du Maurier had three drawings, and Keen two, in every number. The admission of many artists' work makes the paper far more interesting — to me, at least ; and, though there are many drawings without technical merit and without humour, there are many others which make atonement. The influence of Mr. Raven Hill and Mr. Phil May seems salutary. They deal with jokes which depend on illustration — physical jokes, or jokes of character — and they neglect, rightly, third-rate quips of conversation, which form the staple of most artists on the other comic papers. " She : ' Who discovered the circulation of the blood ? '— He : ' A Johnny called Harvey ! '— She : ' Then who discovered Harvey's sauce ? ' " I have invented this as a fair sample of the jests in the more modern comic papers, or in the sad enclosure which serious papers set aside for purposes of mirth. Whether such jests require, or are in any way strengthened by a picture of a *décolletée* girl sitting in the shadow of a standard-lamp, with a bald man bending over the back or her chair, is a question on which I have already made up my mind.

The ordinary complaint against *Punch* seems to be that he has lost the two last letters of his name, and is merely the mouthpiece through which Mr. Burnand forces an old-fashioned and discredited form of humour. For my own part I have never sympathised with Dr. Johnson's view of the pun and its maker, and I have often admired the feats of H. J. Byron. Mr. Burnand has made many good puns in his day, and is still making good puns, nor has he any reason to be ashamed of them. A good pun, properly used, is one of the best bells in the jester's cap. Why its tinkle should be received, in all places and on all occasions, with groans of mock despair,

I have never been able to understand. But it is a pity
that Mr. Burnand should enlarge it to the size of a muffin-
bell and let it drown the whole carrillon. Perhaps he
knows his own business best. I have no wish to be pon-
derous and dictatorial. I do not consider, as his mentors
seem to consider, that he has in *Punch* a sacred trust of
National Humour. Nor am I so foolish as to suppose
that any diatribe will cure him of a phase of fun to which
he has, at length, exclusively devoted himself. I prefer
him as he was when he wrote that delightful work of
humour and insight, that epic farce, " Happy Thoughts."
But, being no magician, I do not expect him to produce
another " Happy Thoughts" at my bidding. In point
of fact, Time, not Mr. Burnand, has been the bane of
Punch. Satire should be irresponsible, tilting at the
strong and the established as well as at the momentary
follies of the day. When *Punch* was young, he had
the courage of his own levity. But *Punch* is old now,
pompous and respectable, exemplary in all relations of
life. No more does he bob wickedly from side to side,
banging everything with his cuddled stick. He grins
and squeaks and bludgeons only in the cause of law and
order, and is most polite to the hangman. He has become a national institution.

25

Yes! scoff at this comic paper as you will, it is as much a national institution as the *Times*. It is no longer the force it was once, but its position is yet strengthened with every year. You cannot root it out. Try to take it in good humour. If you cannot laugh with it, as I do often, laugh lightly at it, as you laugh lightly at its rival in Printing House Square. Blowitz and Mr. Smalley, Mr. Lang and Mr. Humphrey Ward — to say nothing of such outside humorists as Pigott — all these amuse you gently, pleasantly. Why be so angry with poor little Bouverie Street? Come! make the best of it. It is your own dulness that has made comic papers necessary. You are of a nation which can't laugh at large and must needs have certain specified places and occasions for its mirth. You find nothing funny in Mr. Balfour. You take Mr. Asquith quite seriously. But you split your sides at the mere name of Ashmead-Bartlett. Those of you who are journalists put anything funny that they may have to say at the beginnings of their articles, and then start afresh with a " but seriously." As if — but I could never explain. Only remember this, that you are very dull dogs, who do not deserve comic papers half so good as *Punch* and the *Times*.

ACTORS

One never hears any writer or painter declaring that he has made an inviolable rule never to read a criticism of his own work. One cannot imagine any artist, save an actor or a singer, trampling a press-notice under foot, or pasting it on his bed-post. How is it, one wonders, that the swords of the dramatic and of the musical critics are so keen and terrible, their roses so very precious ? Assume not idly that actors and singers have no faith in their own work, nor scoff at them as being creatures of a too high stomach. Try rather, try soberly, to perceive what circumstances of their art make these men and women strangely sensitive. When you have found in what respect the practice of their art differs from the practice of other arts you will perhaps have found, also, the secret of their difference from other artists. The writer's work is given to you between the covers of

a book ; the painter's on a piece of flat canvas ; the actor's
in the lineaments of his own face, the port of his own
body, the various inflections of his own voice.   In criticising his work you criticise, also, him.   Academically,
you may object that what you really criticise is nothing
but his work, his impersonation.   Academically, you
may be quite right.   But that is not the point.   The
actor, having to devote all his time to the development of
his emotions, is the least logical creature in the world,
and the least likely to be comforted by nice distinctions.
He cannot detach himself, as you detach him, from his
work.   Very silly of him, but, when you come to consider
it, quite natural !   So far as he is concerned — and
I am here concerned with him and his feelings —
" in criticising his work, you criticise, also, him."
Wonder not at his sensitiveness !

The Actor's medium is himself.   If some such obvious
formula were more remembered, the silly denunciations,
directed against actors from this or that quarter, on this or
that ground, might be far fewer.   Many people have, for
instance, been terribly shocked by the internecine feuds
of the theatre.   There is more jealousy, say they, among
actors than among any other artists.   They seem to have
forgotten singers, but I need not dispute their proposition.

30

Merely would I submit my obvious formula. Writers and painters are not free from jealousy, and their jealousy is but the less poignant because it is vicarious. They envy one another through one another's work. Actors envy one another.

The charitable influence of my formula is indeed manifold. Ponder my formula ! It must soften the most rasping accuser when he declares that actors are vulgarly discontent with their mere art and are always flooding the newspapers with details of their private lives. It is because actors, in the pursuit of their art, display *themselves*, that the public takes a keen interest in all their circumstances. You must blame, not the actors, but the public. Even supposing (which is foolish) that these "personal paragraphs" are generally inspired by their subjects, they would not be printed unless the public wished to read them. As a matter of fact, actors are no more desirous of irrelevant fame than are any other artists. It is the public which wishes quite naturally, to know all about them. The journalists, quite naturally, seek to gratify the public.

No one, of course, could deny that the dramatist suffers by reason of the actor's great vogue. Strictly speaking, the actor is but one of the media of dramatic art.

31

Being a live medium, he occupies what is, speaking strictly, a false position. The history of the drama in all its rises and declines is the history of the dramatist's sure eclipse by the actor. At first, the actor was but an inanimate medium, a masked convention. Æschylus had nothing to fear from him, though it may have been with a certain prescience of danger that he became, like our Shakespeare, his own protagonist. But, as time went on, the Athenians began to listen not merely to the words, but also to the manner of their recital. One actor was preferred to another by reason of his ampler gesture or his more significant appeal. We know that, in the decadence, he overshadowed the dramatist, and had plays " written round " him, quite in the modern way. Even as now, the dramatist was greatly annoyed. Even as then, the dramatist is quite helpless. He may rail against the actor, but he can avail against him no more than could Frankenstein against his own monster. The public, for whom the dramatist must needs write, in whose sight is the actor, pays its homage, quite naturally, to the actor. The poor, groaning dramatist must needs accommodate himself to the victorious, oppressive, indispensable middleman. You may shed a tear for him, but you cannot, in view of my formula, blame his middleman (or live

medium) for undue selfishness.   Like the convivial Porson,
when he could not light his bedroom candle with an extin-
guisher, you must "damn the nature of things."

Ponder my formula !   The actor's art is evanescent,
and he must needs, therefore, be rather hectic in his
desire for fame.   Good books and good pictures are
monuments, which, once made, are always there and
may take fresh garlands ; but the actor's finest impersonation, repeated night after night, is a thing of no
substance, exists not but from his lips, perishes with
him.   Other artists can afford to wait.   It is not only
that they, as men who work not in the actual presence of
the public, value praise less highly ; it is also that their
art will endure.   For them the immediate verdict is not
irrevocable.   Time turns their rude public into a polite
posterity.   But it is " now or never " with the actor.
One knows how the gayest assemblage of youth may be
chilled by a reference to Macready or Edmund Kean.
Theatrical reminiscence is the most awful weapon in the
armoury of old age.   I am sure that much of the respect
which we pay to an elderly man is due to our suspicion
that he could avenge any slight by describing the late
Charles Matthews in *Cool as a Cucumber*.   It is curiously
exasperating to hear about a great actor whom we have

3

not seen. So far from honouring, we abominate, his memory. Actors are like pet-birds. When a pet-bird dies, there may be, for those who knew it in the day of its song and its ruffling plumage, some poor comfort in the sight of its stuffed body. For others, there is only a sense of depression. The most unsuccessful "super" on the stage may always console himself with the thought that he is, at least, a cut above David Garrick.

"Into the night go one and all." But the gods are not ruthless. They have been kind to these players. We need not weep. In their day, these players are blest supremely. What other artists, save singers, can match their laurels? Their art dies with them, but I think that in the immediateness, the directness of their fame, they are supremely recompensed. Great writers, great painters, must needs suffer many years of insult or of neglect. Most often, when the tardy pæan is sung in their honour, they are too old or too bitter to be gratified by its sound. Nor is the pæan, even if they still care to hear it, so loud and so near as to the actor. Mr. Meredith does not receive one "call" at the end of any chapter, soever noble. When Mr. Whistler puts the finishing touches to a paper-lithograph, soever exquisite, even Mr. Joseph Pennell does not clamber upon the

window-sill and throw in a bouquet. Yet may both
Mr. Meredith and Mr. Whistler be accounted lucky.
Artists, not less great than they, have died without honour,
consoled only by the sure knowledge that their work will
survive gloriously. Their work does, indeed, survive,
but it is not immortal. Even the writings of William
Shakespeare will perish in the next ice-age. The whole
history of this world is but as a moment in eternity, and
happy is that man whose fame is the accompaniment of
his own life. Such a man is the actor. Do not grudge
him his honours. Do not blame him for his love of
them. Ponder my formula, " and, look you! mock him
not !"

MADAME TUSSAUD'S

To plume one's self on a negative virtue, is surely the cheapest form of self-righteousness, and I am not puffed up when I declare that I never was "one of those miserable males" who are ever seeking "sensations" and "experiences." Indeed, I have often suspected that these seekers are but the figment of certain philosophic brains. We all, naturally, have moments of boredom and the desire for diversion. In such a moment, lately, I myself did stray beyond the portal of a scarlet edifice in the Marylebone Road and did wander among wax-works. My visit may have been a "sensation" or an "experience," or both, but it was not at all nice. In future I shall stick to *ennui*.

What is it that pervades this congress of barren effigies? Why is their atmosphere so sinister, so subtly exhaustive? For all creatures, it is said, life ebbs lowest and death's

meridian is in those chill, still intervals before the sun's
relapse or resurrection. I can well imagine that no in-
valid, laid in either interval among these wax-works,
could survive for many minutes. They frightened me, I
remember, when I was a little child and was taken to see
them as a treat. In a sense, they frightened me again, yes-
terday. But my fear, when I came among them, did not
arise from any notion that they were real men and women,
bewitched into an awful calm. I could not have cried
to be taken home. Nay, I could not tear myself from
their company. Powerless of escape, as in a dream, I
must needs wander on, pausing before each one of those
cadaverous and ignoble dolls, hating the tallowy faces and
glass eyes that stared back at me ; the rusty clothes ; the
smooth, nailless, little hands. I wished to Heaven I had
never come into the place, yet must I needs stay there.
The orchestra, playing lively tunes, did but intensify the
gloom and horror of the exhibition. One would prefer
no music in a sarcophagus. Why were they ranged here,
these dolls? What fascination had they? They were
not life-like. They gave me no illusion.

I remembered how Ouida, in one of her earlier books,
had told us of one who came to the dim hall of some
Florentine villa, and, gazing round at the pagan statues

that were there, had fancied himself in the presence of
the immortal gods, and had abased himself before them.
Could any man, I wondered, entering Madame Tussaud's
initial chamber, fancy that the old Kings and Queens of
England had come to life? Mrs. Markham being his sole
authority for most of their faces, he would not be ham-
pered by any positive conceptions. For aught one knows,
Richard Cœur de Lion may have had some such face as
yonder person on the daïs, and King Stephen's image may
be the image of King Stephen. But oh, what stiff and inadequate absurdities! That fatuous puppet, called Mr.
Gladstone, in the next room, is scarcely less convincing.
And even when the familiar features of some man or woman
have been moulded correctly, how little one cares, how
futile it all seems! The figures are animated with no spark
of life's semblance. Made in Man's image, they are as
Man to God. Even from that elaborately set scene, rep-
resenting a Drawing Room at the Court of St. James's,
one can draw no possible illusion. True that the Royal
personages, of whose models it is composed, are better
subjects for ceraceous art than are any humbler folk. The
high remoteness of their life tends to clear them of obvious
vivacity, and these wax-works are apt travesties of faces
whose Olympian calm is unmingled with Olympian con-

templativeness. But even this crowd of models is a failure. See how each figure stands solitary! It is only those imperceptible nerve-currents, passing from one being to another, that can create a homogeneous scene.

Though these wax-works are made in so close an imitation of life, they have, indeed, less verisimilitude than the outcome of any fine art. They are most nearly akin with statuary, I suppose, in that they are themselves a form of plastic art. But statuary, as Pater pointed out, in a pregnant (if rather uncouth) sentence, moves us to emotion, " not by accumulation of detail, but by abstracting from it." I think that wax-works fail, because they are not made within any of those " exquisite limitations " of colour, texture, proportion, to which all visual arts must be subjected. Life, save only through conventions, is inimitable. The more closely it be aped, the more futile and unreal its copy. Well! and herein, perhaps, lies the secret of that enervation which wax-works do produce in many of their beholders. Good painting and good sculpture inspire us with some illusion, thus compensating us for what were otherwise the fatigue of gazing at them. But the best wax-works can only be regarded as specimens of ingenuity, mysterious and elaborate, always abortive. One marvels not that Æneas wept when he saw Troy's fall frescoed on the walls of Carthage. But could Louis Napoleon, coming up from Chislehurst and visiting Madame Tussaud's, have turned away, from the presentment of his lost pomp, with so terrible a heart-cry as " *Quæ regio in terris nostri non plena laboris* " ? I can hardly suppose that any one who ever saw his own wax-work did not feel mortified and sickened. I can imagine a man being haunted, for the rest of his life, by the knowledge that a ghastly double of himself is standing, all day long, over a number, to be gazed at and " looked out " in the catalogue — is standing there, all night long, in the dark. Is the condemned murderer, I wonder, ever appalled by the thought of his sure survival under Madame's· roof? Does he ever realise that, soon after he, poor wretch, has been slung down to eternity, another figure will be propped up in the Chambet of Horrors ?

Such were the speculations that filled my brain, as I roamed morbidly around the exhibition. Though with every moment my vitality seemed to be ebbing lower and lower, though I cursed myself bitterly for being there, I could not tear myself from that gaunt hierarchy of tongueless orators, patriots without blood, and kings whose insignia are coloured glass. The unreality of everything oppressed me, in brain and body, with an indescribable lassitude. I felt dimly that the place was evil, everything in it evil. Life was a sacred thing — why had it been profaned here, for so many years? Whence came this hateful craft? With what tools, in what workshop, who, for whose pleasure, fashioned these obscene images? Images? Yes, of course, they were images. . . . But why should Garibaldi and those others all stare at me so gravely? Had they some devil's power of their own, some mesmerism? It flashed upon me that, as I watched them, they were stealing my life from me, making me one of their own kind. My brain seemed to be shrinking, all the blood ceasing in my body. I would not watch them. I drooped my eyelids. My hands looked smooth, waxen, without nerves. I knew now that I should never speak nor hear again, never move. I took a dull pride, even, in the thought that this was the very frock-coat in which I had been assassinated. . . . With an effort, I pulled myself together. Looking neither to the right nor to the left, I passed, through that morgue of upstanding corpses, to the entrance, down the marble staircase, out into the street. . . . Ah! it was good to be in the street!

GROUPS OF MYRMIDONS

It is a custom of the little clubs at Oxford to be photographed in every Summer Term. Some of them are antique enough to have existed before photography, and so the port, lineaments, and costume of their first members have gone unrecorded for their pious successors. But the club which claimed me had been initiated in days not so remote ; it dated, indeed, only from a decade which had seen, mourned, and forgotten the demise of the daguerreotype. Our club-room was a gallery of " groups " that told the full story of the past and illuminated with the pale rays of sentiment every page of our worn minute-book. Often, as I sat there, gazing round at those records of forgotten faces and modes discarded, my heart was softened towards photography. Surely, in some dark corner of every camera, there lurks a good fairy who enchants every plate as it is exposed. The enchantment

47

may not be, is not, obvious at first — it does not make the developed plate less hideous, less harshly mechanical. Yet the enchantment is there, nevertheless, and, after the lapse of years, it fills the photograph with a curious grace. The very coarseness and crudity of the process are turned to good use. In very virtue of its unintelligent realism, an old photograph gains a pathos which is to be found in old pictures. When we look at an old picture, be it bad or good, our minds turn to him by whom, rather than to him of whom, it was painted. But, while the painter always obtrudes himself on us in his work, and there is no escaping him, who in the world ever thinks about a photographer ? It is because it was done in an instant, that every " group " seems so real and, despite the conventionality and stiffness of its attitudes, so natural. We know what a Babel of talk and laughter had been suspended only an instant before, and how it burst forth again with double force an instant later, when the camera had done its duty. The " groups " of my old club are things snatched from the very heart of Oxford. There is symbolism in the fact that nearly all of them have the same background — the window of a certain room on the ground floor of the New Buildings. The men vanish, and their places are filled by others. Whiskers and velveteens give way gradually to flannels and smooth faces. But "wines" are conducted with the same ceremonial as when *Up in a Balloon, Boys!* and *Have you seen the Shah!* were the liefest ditties. Bonfires are eternally renewed in the same grey quadrangles and are danced round in the same old fashion. Windows are smashed with relentless regularity, though their frames last for ever. The dawn creeps through them and still finds young Bacchanals cursing one another, with the same old freedom, over unlimited loo. Aristotle, with his Ethics, and Plato, with his Republic, cudgel the brains of every successive generation. Academic gowns are cut exactly as they were when men wore them over doublets and trunk-hose. The youngest freshman will be gathered, hereafter, to his fathers, and on that night Great Tom will still be droning the hundred-and-one strokes he droned on the night when the hoariest of the dons was born into the world. No! Oxford never changes. It is well that the undergraduates, the bits of coloured glass in the kaleidoscope, do not realise their transience. Every wall frowns down on them, but they pay no heed. They are full of youth and buoyancy and self-importance — masters of the whole place. Certainly these old photographs are pregnant with irony and with pathos.

They are eloquent as the walls themselves. See how the President always wears a very grave aspect, befitting his tremendous office, and sits in the middle of the group, facing the camera with arms imperially folded !

Where are they, these leaves which the unsparing wind has scattered ? Where are they, the outcast citizens of this gay and tiny commonwealth, these old " Myrmidons " ? O *male dilapsos*, how, in what real warfare, are they, who loitered here in Capua, faring now ? In the Book of Fate (*q. v. passim*), the name and address, the past and future, of every one of them, I doubt not, are duly entered. But, for me, as for all who have never dipped into that fascinating work of reference, there is a pleasure in studying these old groups, in guessing the character of every member from his port and lineaments, and learning in the light of his peculiar costume the vain whims of Fashion. In my time, it was seldom that any of these old members came among us. The lapse of less than a lustre means a new generation in Oxford, and, after the departure of all his comrades' comrades, Oxford is but a husk of barren and bitter-sweet memories to its revisitor. Now and again, however, some wistful, bearded stranger would appear in our midst, revealing himself as one of our own order, and would dine at the

50

house-dinner on Sunday. We respected him as a man of the world ; he envied us for what we were. But our jokes were as incomprehensible to him, I fancy, as were his anecdotes tedious to us. We were very polite to him indeed. But "young barbarians" are far too happy to be sentimental, and their hearts do not go out readily to their forerunners. They know not Joseph, and they don't want to know him. For myself, I rather liked Joseph, and would listen with real pleasure to his reconstruction of the past, and encourage him to tell me of those whose aspects the photographer had handed down to me. Thus, with the help of an occasional Joseph, I came to know a little about some of those old heroes ; how they had bearded the bursar, or bonneted the proctor, or slipped the porter ; how one had since been killed in Afghanistan, and another had been twice married, and another was sheep-farming in Australia and "doing very well; " and another had "gone under," as Joseph had always foreseen. For the most part, they seemed to have cast behind them for ever their days and nights of gambling and hard drinking, and to have become decent, prosperous gentlemen who lived in various counties and met each other seldom. Those others of whom I heard nothing have probably met a similar fate.

I seem to see every one of them as a portly, begaitered man sitting in his study, with the " groups " of his period hanging upon the wall behind him. Of all the Myrmidons, there is only one who has achieved great fame. The " group " in which he appeared (prepare, reader, to be disappointed — I could not afford the cheap jest you are expecting) is dated 1870, and the name inscribed under his figure is a name which has passed already, with its dead bearer, into the political history of our time. There he sits, the future leader of the Fourth Party and of the House itself, among his fellow-Myrmidons — a moody boy, dressed, after the fashion of the day, in a suit of very large checks. His hands are resting on a white hat, and, though the photograph is somewhat faded, one can discern on his upper lip the faint presage of that moustache which was to give the cue to innumerable caricaturists. Except his eyes, there is no feature to distinguish him from any of the young bloods around him. But we, who know now all that Fate was holding for him, cannot but pause, with some stirring of our hearts, under this portrait of him as he was at Merton. How quickly the laurel-branch was to grow for him ; how greatly to flourish ; to be cut off how untimely, yet not before all the leaves on it were withered ! Would one rather be, as, I take it, they who were here portrayed with him still are, sane, healthy, happy, stupid, obscure, or have led, like that young tribune, a short, swift life of triumph and tragedy ?   Which of these two lots would one rather draw ?   Which is the luckier ?   I do not know.

PRETENDING

So far as I can, I avoid that channel of all that is unloveliest in London, the Strand. Some folk profess a charm in it. Me it has repelled always. Was ever anywhere so monotonous a current of harsh faces as flows there? Anxiety, poverty and bedragglement on the pavement, and drivers cursing one another in the blocked traffic; hoarse hucksters on the curb, and debauchees lolling before the drinking-bars — the charm of the scene is rather too abstruse for me, I admit. And if the road be aswill with mud, and the hoofs of every horse be four muddy fountains ; if the day be that most depressing of all days, Saturday, and the hour of that day be five o'clock, when every theatre is vomiting an audience, Heaven help one who does not love the Strand for its own sake. I pressed through the wet mob, and, with a blind instinct for safety, tore myself out of it at a

57

corner that was labelled " Wellington Street." I stood
for a moment, composing myself. Then I walked slowly
up this way of sanctuary. At the stage-door of the
Gaiety Theatre loitered the solitary, melancholy figure
of a young man. The figure had been dressed with
pathetic care. A crooked stick hung from one arm, and
an eyeglass was screwed into the face. The hat, which
was worn at a raffish angle, had evidently been medicated
with some oily nostrum. The scarf-pin had been bought
from a hosier. The boots had that blue and blotchy
surface which means varnish on common leather. In the
coat was a cheap bunch of Parma violets. The figure
was " seeing life." It belonged not to the gilded youth,
but was probably some poor City clerk who had gone
by himself, that afternoon, to the pit or perhaps to the
upper boxes, and had now, greatly daring, strolled round
to regard Lais in mufti. That he knew not Lais, that it
was a damp afternoon, that he was going to have a frugal
tea at the Aerated Bread Shop, that he would never take
any true part in the joys which were his aspiration —
these things mattered little to the tragic ass before me.
He was pursuading himself, for a brief span, that his was
a career of brilliant profligacy. He was " making believe." He was quite happy. Insomuch that, until

two of the emerging girls looked at him, nudged each other, and did a contemptuous titter which caused him to walk quickly away, crimson with humiliation, I was rather envious of him. As I watched his retreating figure, I reflected that there is in every fool's paradise an undergrowth of real brambles, and that it is well to be on the side of the angels who stand discreetly without, whilst others rush in quite regardless of their feet. How much better for that young man, had he been content to be, without masquerade, simply himself; content to take the humble pleasures of his own class, without pretending to those pleasures which are meant for men of " luckier birth " ! In such aspiration the Friend of Man may discern something fine, some earnest of equality to come. But, as a matter of fact, class-encroachment, as practised in this country, will bring us no nearer to Socialism ; indeed, it can but strengthen the barriers of class. In England, the poor want to live like the rich. When they shall want the rich to share their poverty, then there may be some possible danger of a Millennium. If he would have his ideas realised, the Socialist must first kill the Snob. As yet, he has not even challenged him. When he does, I shall back the Snob to beat him. I shall be willing to lay very, very long odds.

Every human creature weaves for himself and wears an elaborate vesture of illusion. All of us pretend. And we pretend in order that we may impress others, not ourselves, and our pleasure is proportionate to our success in making others believe us to be something finer than we are. We grudge no time that is wasted, no convenience that is sacrificed to that end. Gregarious animals, we are gluttons for effect, and the pains we take to produce effect are the chief tragedy of our existence. Not long ago, in the high-street of a small suburb, I saw a symbol that was even more tragic than the symbolic young man at the stage-door. I saw a bow-window through which a bust of Minerva gazed down at me. Minerva's back had been turned upon the inmates of the room, not in Divine discourtesy, but by the very inmates. Imagine the back view of a bust! I need not enlarge upon this curious sight. All of us, in our several ways, avert Minerva's head, not, I fear, from any consideration for a wise goddess, nor with any wish to spread wisdom among our neighbours. We do but want to be envied, and for envy we will pay any price. To enjoy, simply, the things that are ours, is a philosophy beyond us. We value them not, save as material for false display, for deception. Be sure that the inmates of the room in the high-street knew nothing of Minerva, that they had made their purchase merely from the vague love of a genteel culture which was not theirs. For what is ours by natural right we care nothing. In our code possession is nine points of ennui, and we delight only in things alien to us. Our young men ape the wisdom and weariness of eld, whilst eld would fain dance, with stiff limbs, to the joyous and silly tunes of adolescence. What we have not, we simulate; and of what we have, we are heartily ashamed. We pull long faces to hide our mirth, and grin when we are most wretched. We are all of us, always, in everything, straining after contraries. Cicero plumed himself on his poor statesmanship, and Congreve was humiliated because Voltaire treated him as a writer rather than as a gentleman, and Gustave Doré, contemptuous of his true gifts, broke his heart in the vain ambition to be a painter. Philosophers make ghastly efforts to be frivolous, and — but I will leave the reader of this essay to complete my antithesis.

AN INFAMOUS BRIGADE

Not many nights ago, as I was hastening through the frost, I saw a strange glamour in the sky. " Is it Tithonus, " I wondered, " shamed forth, at length, by his Lady's taunts ? " The glamour grew. I thought Aurora had followed her Lord, and was beseeching him to return. But a cabman, whom I consulted, told me it was not Tithonus, nor Aurora, but only some wharf burning by the river. I let him drive me there. Through a rattle of dark alleys sped we, through brawls and squalor. Under the red glory of flames that were reduplicated in sky and water, we rested. Than the roaring of those great flames had I yet heard, than their red glory seen, nothing lovelier.

Yet, under my very eyes, there was an organised attempt to spoil this fair thing. Persons in absurd helmets ran about pouring cascades of cold water on the flames. These, my cabman told me, were firemen. I jumped out and, catching one of them by the arm, bade him sharply desist from his vandalism. I told him that I had driven miles to see this fire, that great crowds of Londoners, poor people with few joys, were there to see it also, and I asked him who was he that he should dare to disappoint us. Without answering my arguments, he warned me that I must not interfere with him "in the discharge of his duty." The silly crowd would not uphold me, and I fell back, surreptitiously slitting his water-hose with a penknife. But what could I avail? The cascades around me were ceaseless, innumerable. Every moment dashed up fresh firemen, imprecant on cars, behind wild horses. In less than an hour, all was over. The flames had been surrounded, driven back and stricken, at length, as they lay, cowering and desperate, in their last embers. But, as they died, there leapt from my heart's core a great residuary flame of indignation. It is still burning.

For my friends assure me that beautiful fires are constantly springing up and are never spared. This fire brigade, as it is called, is a regular organisation, winked at, if not openly encouraged, by the municipal authorities. It has its ramifications in all parts of London. It can produce, at five minutes' notice, its hundreds of hired ruffians, such as I saw that night by the river, none hindering them at their work. I know that vandalism is recurrent in all history. In the days of civil strife, our fairest monuments were marred by the fanatics of Cromwell. Athens wept over the Hermacopeia. The cultured Roman saw, as we see, helmeted Goths charging with hoarse threats through the city. But not secretly nor with fear of retribution, not in hostility to us nor in spiritual fervour, are planned the nightly outrages of "Commander" Wells and his merrymen. Ah! we make a poor community. Americans, as yet inferior to us in the appreciation of most fair things, are far more spirited than we are about fires. Many years ago, when all Chicago was afire, the Mayor, watching it from the Lake-Side, exclaimed in a loud voice, "Who will say now that ours is not the finest city in all the world?" I remember, too, that some years ago, on the eve of my departure from Chicago, a certain citizen, who was entertaining me at supper, expressed his great regret that they had not been able to show me one of their fires. And indeed it must be splendid to see those twenty-three story buildings come crashing down in less time than was required to build them up. In Chicago, extinction is not attempted.

Little value is set on bricks and mortar. A fire is enjoyed ; then the building is reproduced and burnt down again at leisure. But we, who pull down, year by year, old inns and almshouses, because they are obsolete in usage, despite their prettiness and their tradition, we, in London, suffer to be saved any wharf or warehouse, however beautiful its encircling flames, however hideous it.

And here is a strange anomaly ! Whilst there are Companies, which honour with gifts of gold and silver, any one whose silly tenement Vesta has deigned to visit, the Law still loads with chains any one who may be found to have planned the happy occasion. I am far from exalting arson to the level of a fine art. Nothing is easier than to be an incendiary. All you want is a box of matches and a sense of beauty. I know, too, that fires have often been made for unworthy ends, for the gratification of revenge or, even, personal vanity. Nero set light to Rome that he might divert the ears of the musical critics from his indifferent fiddling, and fires, I am told, are mysteriously frequent in the little Duchy of Saxe-Coburg Gotha. But it is absurd that no distinction is made between motives of self-interest and the desire for a pretty scene. Perpend ! I stay for a few days in the country. I see some hay-ricks in a field. After dark. I set light to

68

them.   Am I to be punished for doing so ?   Probably, I admit, the rural police would not dream of suspecting me, and would forthwith arrest the last farm-labourer who had been discharged from the place.   But that does not alter the principle of the thing.   I should be sorry that another should suffer for me, but, having done no wrong, I certainly should not give myself up.

Vain, though, to cavil at the follies of the law, as exemplified here and there, until the public has been thoroughly aroused on the general question of its right to the unspoilt enjoyment of fires !   The sentimentalist may prattle of life-saving, but we must think, rather, of the greatest happiness of the greatest number.   And, as a matter of fact, the strongest objection to the fire-brigade may be raised on behalf of those very persons whom it professes to benefit.   Perpend, reader, once more !   You are a householder.   You are sleeping in the dead of night. The insidious savour of smoke awakens you.   You rush out on to the landing, only to find the staircase enveloped in smoke, whose dense volumes are flame-cloven.   Escape is impossible !   You rush back and rouse your wife and children.   In half-conscious terror, they cling to your knees.   It is the most tragic moment of your life.   You feel that the Ministers of Fate have compassed you about, that Death is grinning at you from their ranks and will soon beckon. Already the smoke is curling round you, already . . . The sash of the window is thrown up. In jumps a perfect stranger in fancy dress and proceeds to play snapdragon with you and your wife and children. An anti-climax! The whole scene ruined! You are bundled down a ladder, protesting that an Englishman's house is his castle. Some scores of licensed practical-jokers are below with their squirts, and you are drenched to the skin, as likely as not. Finally, you are put to bed in some neighbour's house. So ends your tragedy, reader.

Not forgetting that before the next dawn breaks your house may be wet ashes and you its unwilling survivor, try now, reader, to take an altruist view. For the fire-brigade is most hateful, not because it invades the sanctity of our home-life, but because it takes constantly from so many citizens their enjoyment of fair things. I know that the fire-brigade is strong. It will die hard. Years hence, it may still be flourishing. But, meanwhile, one should not be idle. I am forming an Artists' Corps, whose aim will be to harass the members of the fire-brigade on all occasions. I am maturing an elaborate system of false alarms, and I shall train my recruits to waylay the enemy in their onrush, seize the bridles of their horses, cut their reins. We, too, shall hold ourselves in readiness to start off at five minutes' notice, but there will be no furious driving, no terrorising of harmless traffic. We shall go about our work in a quiet, gentlemanly manner : servants, not tyrants, of the public. Though at first, necessarily, our organisation will be small, we shall extend it gradually, I hope. We shall, in time, despise mere guerilla warfare and take our stand upon the very field of battle. Each one of us will trail a sinuous hose. It will not be filled with water. It will be filled with oil.

THE SEA-SIDE IN WINTER

I am always fascinated by the thought of a great statesman *en vacance*. How he must love to look from the window of his library and see, not the court-yard of government-offices, but the balustered terrace and the green, familiar undulations of his own park. On the grass, there is no scurry of government-clerks, special messengers, private secretaries, but only the foolish foregathering of the deer. His children are at play on the terrace. His books line the high walls around him. Save that blot of scarlet, his despatch-box, there is nothing to harass him in his quietude. On my table, too, there are but a quill and a few sheets of foolscap. Around me are the usual ornaments of sea-side lodgings. Through a little bay-window I look out over the wide sea. I have looked, so, through many little bay-windows. But, on my heart, I do not distinguish them one from another; they are all as one

75

for me, all symbolise home for me, quietude and home.
A fine park, seen through an oriel window, is for its in-
heritor, and you shall search vainly for my name in the
Landed Gentry. But all the green acres of the sea are
mine, and I cast a territorial eye over them. The fish-
ing-boats that browse on them are my deer. My balustered terrace is the Parade. Yes! in whatever sea-
side town I find myself I am filled with a quiet pride, a
restfulness of possession. With the first breath of its
wet salt, all the stains of the town are purged, the
vapours blown quite away. I am, like Sir Willoughby
Patterne, "not a poet," and so the sea does not move
me, as it moves Mr. Swinburne, to superb dithyrambs,
nor send me searching, as it sends Mr. William Watson
searching, for adjectives long enough to express unquali-
fied approval. For me, the sight of it is sacramental, not
because it has any power to overwhelm my soul, but
because it alone can restore that sense of self-importance,
which London takes from me. For me, θάλαττα κλύζει
πάντα κακά, indeed.

I like it best in the dead season of Winter. The little
towns that dot the south coast and have their absurd season in August or September, are pathetic in all other
months, but especially, I think, in those wintry months

when all the echoes of their late gaiety are so long dead
and so far from re-awakening. I am fond of coming in
Winter to a place whose Season I do already know.
Last August, I was here, in little L———. February finds
me here again, but almost alone, and dressed like Ovid in
exile, and with the snows of yester year hanging over me
in a grey sky. Hardly a sign is there of human habita-
tion, though the shops are still open, with the same
names over them. The same small crescents, so Early-
Victorian and demure, still face the sea. Their every
window bears that monotonous plea, "Apartments."
The Parade stretches out before me, a white streak of
desolation, flecked with a few figures. There stands
the blind man by his telescope, through which no one,
not even in the height of the Season, ever looked. One
or two old gentlemen, perfectly betweeded, walk with a
rather furtive jauntiness that is begotten of gout and the
desire to conceal gout. They doff their hats gallantly
to the one or two lady-residents who pass by, hardy,
strapping creatures with black straw hats and crooked
walking-sticks. Christmas roses ! Yes, and there are
the orphans, a long double-file of small queerly-dressed
girls, carrying spades and pails, just as they did in the
Summer. They are going down to their dreary task of

building. If one of them tried to escape, I suppose she would be shot down like a Dartmouth convict. And here are the tarred lobster-pots lying in the road, and that is where the town-band used to play every morning, and there sang the comic singers in a crowd of children. I sit down in one of those glass shelters, which were once, and will be again hereafter, so full of nurses, and I light the cigarette of melancholy. Another, a more affluent, girls' school soon files past me. The girls are chattering briskly, and the wind waves their hair behind them, as they walk. It was their holiday, I suppose, when I was here in the Summer. What a grotesque governess backs the procession !

After the first day or so, my melancholy leaves me. The very loneliness of the place does but accentuate my proprietary sense. From the midst of all this lifeless monotony I stand out, a dominant and most romantic personage. Were I in London, who would notice me, no prince there ? Even here, in the Season, I had but a slight pre-eminence over other visitors. But now I need but show myself to create a glow of interest and wonder. The blind man, standing by his telescope, knows my tread, and tries, I think, to picture my appearance. The old gentlemen see in me the incarnation of splendid youth ; the shop-

people, a dispenser of great riches ; the school-girls, a
prodigy of joyous freedom from French verbs. I could
not have levied these tributes in the month of August.
Nor could I have relished so heartily as now the simple
pleasures which the sea-side always can afford. Everything is delightful. I look forward to everything. As I
walk Stationwards for the morning papers, I can scarcely
contain my great interest in current events ; and, later,
when I have learnt all that is troubling that city whose
happy exile I am, how pleasant to lean over the Parade's
railing and watch Neptune's troupe of performing waves !
I know not how these wild things have been trained,
but to see them as they advance, *à chasse roulée,* the
little ones a-front, the big ones following, I could almost
fancy they were dancing for their own pleasure, rather
than from any fear of the trident. Neptune is the *doyen*
of our showmen, but, in spite of his immense popularity,
he is always introducing new features. His waves were
at Broadstairs, not long ago, when I was there. They
were actually carrying up sea-weed in their white teeth
and arranging it in strips on the sand. When I threw
them a pebble, they curled over and bowed to me.
Here, too, some of the bigger ones have been taught
to leap over the Parade. I wish Neptune would bring

79

them to London. Perhaps, however, they would be less amusing there. Every pleasure is here so generously magnified. I do even enjoy my meals — the simpler the food, the more Gargantuan my appetite. I wonder how I can ever have sat out the tedious comedy of dinner, when it is possible to enjoy that variety-entertainment, high tea, in which ham and scones and shrimps and hard-boiled eggs and honey all take their short, delightful "turns." And then, when one is well satisfied, to emerge, not into the garish Strand, but upon the dark sea-front, and to feel, as one notes the shimmer of the moon across the waters, that the lamp-posts are shining with a grotesquely similar radiance across the mud of every thoroughfare in London.

At the end of a week, spent in such a place as this, where the focus of all things has been deranged for my pleasure, I have so far forgotten London as a place of real dwelling that I have no great dread of my return. My holiday is over, but I am so permeated with happiness that my departure is not grievous. My self-conceit, so carefully fostered here, has grown out of all bounds, and I, who came here as a mere proprietor, leave like an Imperial Guest. Before I am driven to the railway-station, with sea-breezes for my escort, I present my landlady with a daguerreotype of myself, signed by my own hand.

IF I WERE ÆDILE

Since first met, in Spring Gardens, a certain mischievous and meddlesome body of men, we have heard much of the proposed improvement of London — "betterment" is the very expressive word they use. "London clean! London beautiful!" is their cry, fraught with sinister meaning to those who understand. As yet, indeed, they have not done very much harm. But that is not their fault. From the first they have been brimful of horrible intentions. Even Hampstead was not sacred to them. "An uncouth heath!" they would seem to have exclaimed. "This must be seen to." And so the dear wilds of Hampstead, its knolls and ridges and tiny precipices, began to be levelled, bettermented, brought up to date. And the pale refugees from London, who love to clamber there, never but wondering that so fair and strange an upland overhangs the city of their

travail, found smooth walks and strong railings set there,
and flower-beds, far superior to the furze-bushes. Then
the fist of Public Opinion was shaken so angrily that the
Councillors quaked before it and, snatching up their pick-
axes and their two-foot rules, their trowels and their
packets of seeds, went stumbling away down the hill.
Awhile, they lay low. But soon they came up on Chel-
sea Reach, smiling ; hoping, doubtless, that the mists
which do ever shroud that dear place, sanctified by so
many painters and poets, would hide their embankment
till it were complete. Somebody saw their ominous
figures groping along the bank. An alarm was raised.
The plans of the embankment were seized. Bohemia's
fist was shaken to its foundations. The Councillors scuttled away, growling. And, ever since, they have been
much more careful. They have learnt that sacred suburbs
must not be lightly desecrated, and they while away
their time with threats against the Metropolis, which has
fewer champions. Lo here ! is the burning question of
the Strand. The Councillors have popped across the
Channel and come back raving about Boulevards. If one
German Baron could do so much for Paris, what could
not a lot of earnest Radicals do for the London ? Lo
there ! is the burning question of Piccadilly. The Radi-

cals are ashamed of Piccadilly, so narrow, so irregular is it. But they point the finger of righteous pride at that new railing, which bounds the courtyard of Devonshire House. The old wall of brown brick, this railing's predecessor, they had long regarded as a grave insult to themselves and the democracy. Had it threatened the lives of the foot-passengers, they would have had it down in less than no time ; but it was solid. All they could do was to stamp around, calling it " grimy " and " most unsightly." People confessed that they had never thought of it in that light, but that, since their attention had been drawn to it, they certainly did think the wall was most hideous. Radical editors stood under it and blew their trumpets for its downfall. And the Duke of Devonshire did not say to them, as he should have said, ' Be damned to you ! '' but gave them a railing.

Well ! I am not of the stuff which stems the tide of democracy. A delicate and Tory temperament precludes me from conversation with Radicals. But I did, during the agitation I have described, address to them, through their *Daily Chronicle,* an oblique remonstrance. I pointed out to them that noblemens' courtyards were a very curious, very charming survival, and that their arrogant mystery should not be disturbed. Alas ! I paid the penalty of the *poseur*. My letter was taken as a joke. The only passage in it which seemed to impress the Radicals, was a little quibble to the effect that the wall should stand, if only to veil the ugliness of the house behind it. They seemed to think there was something in that. Beauty is not indispensable to architecture. The very ugliest of houses is often, διὰ τὸ μέγεθος, impressive, even apart from its associations, and can arouse in those who see it emotions of profound awe. I will not enumerate the many buildings in London, which, destitute as they are both of beauty and of association, one yet values for the impressive dignity of their aspect. Devonshire House, moreover, is full of grim style. Its disclosure to the street does not offend me, except for this reason : that there were many fine houses in Piccadilly and but one fine, invisible courtyard.

Radical eyebrows and Radical shoulders rise, I am sure, at this declaration. I wish it were not impossible for me to receive the Radicals personally and speak to them. A deputation, in my room, would learn much. It would hear these words : " You are all of you very excellent, very ignorant, men. Meaning well in your schemes of ' Betterment,' you know nothing whatever about architecture. Style, character, beauty, tradition, are unintel-

ligible to you. London is not a beautiful town, I know,
but its aspect has fine qualities, to be revered. These
qualities are the result of certain historical contrasts between the nobility, the burgesses, and the mob. You
chafe at these contrasts. The razure of the Duke of
Devonshire's wall is a perfect symbol of your policy.
You think that, by the removal of old barriers, by the
creation of open spaces, you can rid London of its som-
breness, make it bright and cheerful and 'Frenchy,'
make it beautiful. If London were swept away by another
fire, and you were allowed to rebuild it, you would take
Paris for your model, would you not? That shows you
have no sense of national character, of the inherent som-
breness in Englishmen, which gay surroundings would but
make ridiculous. You would rebuild London on some
uniform plan, would you not? I daresay, then, you
admire New York. You have never been there? You
should go. Meanwhile, in London, there is no prospect
of a holocaust, and you can but tinker. In the country,
you inveigh against the parks of noblemen and claim
them for the public. In London you call noblemen's
courtyards 'grimy.' Well, you are powerful. Cripple
these noblemen, if you must, with Death Duties and give
their revenues to the mob. But spare them, and spare

us, the fine flavour of their seclusion. It gives me no
pleasure to address you. Yet, now that I am doing so, I
will extend my speech, slightly. I am told that you are
gradually destroying the tripartite nature of the English
people ; that you are drawing down the aristocracy, and
drawing up the mob, into the middle class. Let me tell
you, indeed, you probably know, that the equality of
man is an ideal which cannot be fulfilled. Some kind of
chaos you may, in time, establish. The laws of contrast, which govern mankind, will very soon reduce that
chaos to order. A new tyranny will take the place of
the old. That is all. And the old tyranny of birth,
which is also the tyranny of style, will be mourned bitterly, when it has passed away. I will answer no
questions, hear no speeches. The deputation will now
withdraw.''

Some kind of authority is, doubtless, needed to direct
the architectural changes in a great city. That persons
so inept as they to whom I have spoken this imaginary
address should be intrusted with any fraction of such
authority, is an æsthetic scandal. Nor can we congratu-
late ourselves on the Ayrtons and Lefevres, who have
been our Ædiles. I should be glad to see the powers of
the First Commissioner of Works greatly extended, and

his office held by an artist, not by a party-hack. The functions of such a minister would, of course, be rather to protect than to destroy or to construct. If I were chosen for the post, I should exercise little originality, much reverence ; recognising that Time is an architect, with whose work one should not lightly tamper. A new building I should judge, not on its own merits, nor according to my own preferences, but in reference to its surroundings, also, and to its owner. If, for instance, I had been Ædile in '94, and the plans of Mr. Beit's house in Park Lane had been duly submitted to me, I should have passed them readily. I know that the house looks rather absurd, now that it is finished. *On dirait* some little bungalow wafted by an evil magician from the shores of Bexhill-on-Sea. But in its way it is interesting — who could ever have fancied that a millionaire would be so unassuming ? And, in a hundred years, it may even look pretty. Nor does it spoil the aspect of Park Lane, whose charm, indeed, depends upon variety.

On the other hand, I should never have allowed Lord Rosebery to thump down that loud, scarlet note among the brown and green harmonies of Berkeley Square. I should keep a very jealous guard upon Berkeley Square. With its perfect tone, its quietude, with Lord Bath's dolphins, Lord Lansdowne's long wall, the old and pleasant anomaly of Gunter's, it is an ineffably distinguished place. Grosvenor Square is so wild a motley, that I would make no rules there. But in St. James' Square, that superb example of all that is best, and greatest, and most gloomy in our architecture, I would be a despot indeed. The receivers of money, who have occupied so great a part of it, I would ruthlessly drive forth, and in their empty houses I would reinstate the impoverished noblemen, whose ancestors once lived there. Who cares that the place is insanitary? History haunts it. The ghosts of many centuries gather upon its doorsteps. Every window has the pathos of a frame wherefrom some great picture has been torn. From one, Nell Gwynne waved her naughtily-embellished fingers. From another, poor Caroline dropped her clumsy curtseys to the mob. At that window, yonder, not so long since, sat " The Rupert of Debate," glowering through his spectacles and cursing his swathed foot. . . . Yes, I would be a real despot in St. James' Square.

As I have suggested, my functions would be mainly negative. But there are some things in London which I should destroy. There is one especially fatuous kind of ornamentation which I should spare not for one moment. I should make very short work of any Victorian statues I saw standing about. There are many of them. There is no escape from them. For sculpture is the most obtrusive of all arts. Its elemental grandeur, its breadth of aspect, swiftly impressive, and the archaic hardiness of its material, give it a right *in aëre, in frigore, in imbri.* It was the supreme decoration of great cities. It is the supreme disfigurement of great cities. None but a sculptor and his mother would deny that it is a lost art. And yet, whenever an eminent person dies, we know (nor seem to care) that, within a year or two, his friends will have foisted on some street or square a marble abortion so obscene that no one in any future generation can, by any possibility, forget him. I am the last person to disparage grotesques; but I do not think they are quite a nice means of commemorating our mighty dead. If England, in her old age, is beginning to lose her memory and cannot, without some system of mnemonics, remember the names of her great sons, she had better make up her mind to forget them at once. At any rate, she really must dispense with such ghastly reminders as the work of her modern sculptors. No doubt she will object that statuary is the one kind of art that can be made obvious. But, if I were Ædile, this objection would not move me for one instant. I should point out to her that it is better to sacrifice even memory than to sacrifice personal appearance, and I should direct her to the National Portrait Gallery.

I should make rather a good Ædile. I do not deny that, as a private individual and a caricaturist, passing through Knightsbridge, I have often been grateful for that gilt-splashed effigy of Lord Strathnairn. In Piccadilly Circus, I am often convulsed by the Gilbertian humour of that little Mercury. But official responsibilities would sober me, and, whatever the qualms of my own facetious spirit, all the Victorian statues in London would soon be toppling down. I should unleash my gangs of skilled iconoclasts at the marble feet of every poet and hero, philosopher and philanthropist. Albert the Good would not escape me, nor that vague embryo of Sir Walter Besant, which, even now, on very clear days, we can see towering over the Thames Embankment, nor . . . "Why ! what an ass am I ! " I shall never be Ædile. Statues will continue to bob up around us, till every corner has its side-splitter. And meanwhile, in the alleged poverty of our national defences, it will be comfortable to know that we need not fear Mummius.

92

SIGN–BOARDS

Why do artists no longer paint sign boards for our pleasure? They should really do so. Sign-boards were far more congenial than posters to their talent. No painter of distinction ever succeeds in doing posters. Unable to rid him of his own knowledge, he cannot learn the rather harsh conditions that they impose. But the sign-board is a ground for his very own work. Its function is not, like the poster's function, merely to arrest the casual eye and proclaim a ware, but rather to attract and fascinate one, and to make one, haply, enter the shop it overhangs. Thus is all scope given for a more delicate technique, a subtler fancy. Mere masses of colour, crude intensity of conception, wherewithout posters fail, were quite unnecessary, were inappropriate. The Neo-Romantics, the dalliers with pretty sentiment, would paint admirable sign-boards. I am sure that one painted

95

by Mr. Conder would ensure patronage to the most in-
competent modiste. Mr. Will Rothenstein, again, were
a handy man for the tailors. But all good painters would
do well, after their kind, in an art which yielded triumphs
to Hogarth and Holbein, to Correggio and " Old "
Crome.

Therefore, let not the shopkeepers tarry, but let them
go with gold to the places where artists dwell. That
they should hang out sign-boards is not, surely, an un-
reasonable request. Signs they have never wholly aban-
doned. The chemist's window is still signalised by its
array of lurid vessels, dear to little children. A brazen
sheep droops, even now, over some hosiers' doors, and
a few of those old Highlanders, the least offensive statues
we have, may be seen fingering the snuff-horn, even now.
A survival of mere sentiment ! These signs were invented
for the enlightening of customers, long ago, when few
were scholarly enough to read a superscription. But now,
of course, every one is taught to read. Nor will the survival of these signs stem that abominable torrent of education, which is flooding, but will never fertilise, the land.
" Why then," asks the shopkeeper, " should I spend my
money on a sign-board ? " Sir, I will explain. I do
not ask you to revive those old conventional designs, as

who should hang a green bush before a tavern, what not
and so forth. Adopt, rather, a fanciful and original sign-
board, peculiar to the character of your own wares,
peculiar, also, to the painter of it. From the point of
custom, your money will be well spent. And your board
will, moreover, teach you to chasten your shop-window,
whose ordering you understand so ill. But "shop-
windows," you object, "have made these boards unnecessary. They are attractive enough in themselves."
You are wrong, believe me! Your window is quite
repulsive. But the sign-board, being itself an absolute
symbol, will teach you how very well it is to symbolise,
rather than to parade, your wares. Are you a jeweller?
You fill your window with a garish and unseemly chaos
of all you have : bracelets, sleeve-links, penknives, tiaras —
toute la boutique. Your rival in Paris, even in New
York, is much wiser. He understands the value of a
reticent symbolism. Very little puts he into his window.
What he puts is good. Men and women, beholding,
praise it. Their imagination has been stirred, their appetite whetted for the things that are withheld, and they
long to enter in at the door. Last winter, in the Rue
de la Paix, I saw a jewel-window, sir, that should serve
for an example to you. It was lined with scarlet velvet

and illustrious with electric light. In the very middle of it, lay, like a bomb in a palace, one beautiful black pearl. Had I been rich, I must have entered. Are you a florist? I blame you less for your profusion. For flowers, being things of Nature, do not need any artistic ordering, and your window, with its lilies and forget-me-nots and lilac-branches, is a chance patch of the country, not unwelcome to us. Yet you, also, might expose but one single daffodil, on some days. And as for the crude efforts of your neighbour, the butcher, to create a pastoral atmosphere, I cannot think of them but with utter contempt. Let him put up all his shutters and keep the dreadful secrets of the slaughter-house to himself. Mr. Sydney Cooper shall do him a sign-board. And why should the sea give up its dead to fish-mongers who harrow us with the corpses? And why does the Stereoscopic Company reveal to us the ugliness of everybody in England?

Sign-boards will be to our shop-keepers an object-lesson in this reticent symbolism, as to our painters a new ground for their art, a new source of honest pennies. Above all, they will give a new charm to the town. For not only will shop-windows, under their influence, become beautiful, but the sign-boards themselves, in their long vista, will add to the fair aspect of many streets. In Bond Street, that modish alley, they will have their value, I think. I have seen the old banners that depend from either side of the St. George's Chapel, at Windsor. They have their value.

OUIDA

101

The Democracy of Letters will exasperate or divert you, according to your temperament. Me it diverts merely. It does no harm to literature. Good books are still written, good critics still criticise, in the old, quiet way ; and, if the good books are criticised chiefly by innumerable fools hired to review an imponderable amount of trash, I do not really see that it matters at all. The trash itself is studied, now and again, by good critics and so becomes a spring-board for good criticism, and it were unfair as it were useless, therefore, to shield good books from the consideration of ordinary reviewers. You may call it monstrous that a good writer should be at the mercy of such persons, but I doubt whether the good writer is himself aggrieved. He needs no mercy. And, as a matter of fact, the menaces hurled by the ordinary reviewers, whenever something new or

strange confronts them, are very vain words indeed, and
may at any moment be merged in clumsy compliments.
A good critic — and by that term I mean a cultured man
with brains and a temperament — may at any moment
come by, and, if he praise, the ordinary reviewers, most
receptive of all creatures, will praise also. I was glancing
lately through a little book of essays, written by a lady.
At the end of the book were printed press-notices about
a volume of this lady's book of verse. Among these
gems, and coruscating beyond the rest, was one graven
with the name of Mr. William Sharp: "In its class I
know no nobler or more beautiful sonnet than 'Renounce-
ment;' and I have so considered it ever since the day
when Rossetti (who knew it by heart), repeating it to
me, added that it was one of the three finest sonnets ever
written by women." Such a confession as Mr. William
Sharp's is not to be found in the ordinary press-notice,
but that is merely because the ordinary reviewer is of a
less simple and sunny disposition than our friend, and
speaks not save as one having his own authority. Nevertheless he is in no wise more clever than Mr. Sharp (or
Captain Sumph), and very likely he did not even know
Rossetti. Whether Mr. Sharp liked this sonnet before
he met it under high auspices, is a point which may

never be made clear, but there can be no doubt that the method of the ordinary reviewer is to curse what he does not understand, until it be explained to him. The element of comedy becomes yet stronger if the reviewers be subsequently assured that the explanation was all wrong. Who shall forget the chorus of adulation that rent the welkin for the essays of this very lady whose sonnet Mr. Sharp " so considered " ? Two great writers had greatly praised her. I, humble person, mildly suggested that their praise had been excessive, and gave some good reasons for my opinion. Since then, the chorus has been palpably less loud, marred even by discordant voices. I do not pride myself particularly on this effect; I record it only because it gives a little instance of a great law.

Simpler, more striking, and more important, as an instance of reviewers' emptiness, is the position of Ouida, the latest of whose long novels, *The Massarenes*, had what is technically termed " a cordial reception " — a reception strangely different from that accorded to her novels thitherto. Ouida's novels have always, I believe, sold well. They contain qualities which have gained for them some measure of Corellian success. Probably that is why, for so many years, no good critic took the trouble to praise them. The good critic, with a fastidiousness which is perhaps a fault, often neglects those who can look after themselves ; the very fact of popularity — he is not infallible — often repels him ; he prefers to champion the deserving weak. And so, for many years, the critics, unreproved, were ridiculing a writer who had many qualities obvious to ridicule, many gifts that lifted her beyond their reach. At length it occurred to a critic of distinction, Mr. G. S. Street, to write an " Appreciation of Ouida," which appeared in the *Yellow Book*. It was a shy, self-conscious essay, written somewhat in the tone of a young man defending the moral character of a barmaid who has bewitched him, but, for all its blushing diffidence, it was a very gentlemanly piece of work, and it was full of true and delicate criticism. I myself wrote, later, in praise of Ouida, and I believe that, at about the same time, Mr. Stephen Crane wrote an appreciation of his own in an American magazine. In a word, three intelligent persons had cracked their whips — enough to have called the hounds off. Nay more, the furious pack had been turned suddenly into a flock of nice sheep. It was pretty to see them gambling and frisking and bleating around *The Massarenes*.

Ouida is not, and never was, an artist. That, strangely enough, is one reason why she had been so little appre-

ciated by the reviewers. The artist presents his ideas in
the finest, strictest form, paring, whittling, polishing. In
reading his finished work, none but a few persons note
his artistic skill, or take pleasure in it for its own sake.
Yet it is this very skill of his which enables the reviewers
to read his work with pleasure. To a few persons, artistic
skill is in itself delightful, insomuch that they tend to
overrate its importance, neglecting the matter for the
form. Art, in a writer, is not everything. Indeed, it
implies a certain limitation. If a list of consciously
artistic writers were drawn up, one would find that most
of them were lacking in great force of intellect or of
emotion ; that their intellects were restricted, their emotions not very strong. Writers of enormous vitality never
are artistic : they cannot pause, they must always be
moving swiftly forward. Mr. Meredith, the only living
novelist in England who rivals Ouida in sheer vitality,
packs tight all his pages with wit, philosophy, poetry,
and psychological analysis. His obscurity, like that of
Carlyle and Browning, is due less to extreme subtlety
than to the plethoric abundance of his ideas. He cannot
stop to express himself. If he could, he might be more
popular. The rhapsodies of Mr. Swinburne, again, are
so overwhelmingly exuberant in their expression that no

ordinary reader can cope with them ; the ordinary reader
is stunned by them before he is impressed. When he
lays down the book and regains consciousness, he has
forgotten entirely what it was all about. On the other
hand reticence, economy, selection, and all the artistic
means may be carried too far. Too much art is, of
course, as great an obstacle as too little art ; and Pater, in
his excessive care for words, is as obscure to most people
as are Carlyle and Browning, in their carelessness. It is
to him who takes the mean of these two extremes, to that
author who expresses himself simply, without unnecessary
expansion or congestion, that appreciation is most readily
and spontaneously granted.

Well! For my own part, I am a dilettante, a *petit
maître*. I love best in literature delicate and elaborate
ingenuities of form and style. But my preference does
not keep me from paying due homage to Titanic force,
and delighting, now and again, in its manifestation. I
wonder at Ouida's novels, and I wonder still more at
Ouida. I am staggered when I think of that lurid se-
quence of books and short stories and essays which
she has poured forth so swiftly, with such irresistible
élan. What manner of woman can Ouida be ? A
woman who writes well never writes much. Even

Sappho spent her whole life in writing and rewriting
some exquisite, isolated verses, which, with feminine
tact, she handed down to posterity as mere fragments
of her work. In our own day, there are some ladies
who write a large number of long books, but I am sure
that the "sexual novel" or the "political novel," as
wrought by them, must be as easy to write as it is hard
to read. Ouida is essentially feminine, as much *une
femme des femmes* as Jane Austen or "John Oliver
Hobbes," and it is indeed remarkable that she should yet
be endowed with force and energy so exuberant and indefatigable. All her books are amazing in their sustained
vitality. Vitality is, indeed, the most patent, potent
factor in her work. Her pen is more inexhaustibly pro-
lific than the pen of any other writer; it gathers new
strength of its every dip into the ink-pot. Ouida need
not, and could not, husband her unique endowments, and
a man might as well shake his head over the daily rising
of the indefatigable sun, or preach Malthusianism in a
rabbit-warren, as counsel Ouida to write less. Her
every page is a riot of unpolished epigrams and unpolished poetry of vision, with a hundred discursions and
redundancies. She cannot say a thing once; she must
repeat it again and again, and, with every repetition, so it

seems to me, she says it with greater force and charm. Her style is a veritable cascade, in comparison with which the waters come down at Lodore as tamely as they come down at Shanklin. And, all the while, I never lose interest in her story, constructed with that sound professional knowledge, which the romancers of this later generation, with their vague and halting modes, would probably regard as old-fashioned. Ouida grips me with her every plot, and — since she herself so strenuously believes in them — I can believe even in her characters. True, they are not real, when I think of them in cold blood. They are abstractions, like the figures in early Greek tragedies and epics before psychology was thought of — things of black or white, or colourless things to illustrate the working of destiny, elemental puppets for pity or awe. Ouida does not pretend to the finer shades of civilized psychology. Her men and women of Mayfair are shadows, as I see when I am not under the direct spell of her writing, and she reproduces real life only when she is dealing with childish or half-savage natures — Cigarette the *vivandière*, Redempta the gipsy, Italian peasants, dogs and horses. She cares for the romance and beauty and terror of life, not for its delicate shades and inner secrets. Her books are, in the true sense of the

word, romances, though they are not written in Wardour
Street. The picturesqueness of modern life, transfigured
by imagination, embellished by fancy, that is her *forte*.
She involves her stock-figures — the pure girl, the wicked
woman, the adorable hero and the rest — in a series of
splendid adventures. She makes her protagonist a guards-
man that she may describe, as she alone can, steeple-
chases and fox-hunts and horses running away with
phaetons. Or she makes him a diplomat, like Strath-
more, or a great tenor, like Corèze, or a Queen's messen-
ger, like Erceldoune, or something else — anything so
that it be lurid and susceptible of romance. She ranges
hither and thither over all countries, snatching at all
languages, realising all scenes. Her information is as
wide as Macaulay's, and her slips in local colour are but
the result of a careless omniscience. That she should
have referred to " the pointing of the *digito monstrari*,"
and headed one of her chapters with the words " Thalassis ! Thalassis ! " and made the Queen present at a
Levée, and thrown one or two false side-lights on the
Oxford Eights Week, may seem very terrible to the
dullards who think that criticism consists in spotting mis-
takes. But the fact remains that Ouida uses her great
information with extraordinary effect. Her delight in

beautiful things has been accounted to her for vulgarity
by those who think that a writer "should take material
luxury for granted." But such people forget, or are
unable to appreciate, the difference between the per-
functory faking of description, as practised by the average
novelist — as who should say "soft carpets," "choice
wines," "priceless Tintorettos" — and description which
is the result of true vision. No writer was ever more
finely endowed than Ouida with the love and knowledge
of all kinds of beauty in art and nature. There is nothing
vulgar in having a sense of beauty — so long as you have
it. Ouida's descriptions of boudoirs in palaces are no
more vulgar nor less beautiful than her descriptions of
lakes and mountains.

With their fair, silken moustachios and their glen-
garries and their velvet jackets, Ouida's guardsmen, pegs
for luxury and romance, are vastly stimulating. I should
like to have peered through the cloud of "Turkish"
that did always involve them, and have seen Lord Vaulerois tossing aside a pile of millefleurs-scented notes and
quaffing curaçoa, as he pondered the chances of Peach-
Bloom for the Guards' Steeplechase, or the last mad
caprice of Léla Liette! Too languid, as he lay there on
his divan, to raise the vinaigrette to his nostrils, he was one

who had served his country through more than one cam-
paign on the boiling plains of the Sahara ; he who, in the
palace of a *nouveau riche,* had refused the bedchamber
assigned to him, on the plea that he could not sleep under
a false Fragonard, had often camped *à la belle étoile* in
the waste places of Central Asia ; thrice he had passed
through the D. C. as calmly as he would swim the Hel-
lespont or toss off a beaker of rosy Comet-Wine ; with
his girlish hands that Duchesses envied he had grappled
lions in the jungle, and would think nothing of waiting
for hours, heedless of frost and rain, to bring down some
rocketer he had marked in a warm corner at Crichel or
Longleat. Familiar with Cairene Bazaars as with the
matchless deer-forests of Dunrobin, with the brown fens
round Melton Mowbray as with the incomparable grace
and brilliance of the Court of Hapsburg ; *bienvenu* in the
Vatican as in the Quirinal ; deferred to by Dips and
Décorés in all the *salons* of Europe, and before whom
even Queens turned to coquettes and Kings to comrades ;
careless, carressed, *insouciant ;* of all men the beloved or
envied ; inimitable alike in his grace of person and in the
perfection of his taste ; passing from the bow-windows
of St. James's to the faded and fetid alleys of Stamboul,
from the Quartier Bréda to the Newski Prospect, from

the citron-groves of Cashmere, the gay fuchsia-gardens of
Simla, to the hideous chaos of Illinois, a region scorched
by the sirocco, swept by inextinguishable prairie-fires,
sepultured in the white shrouds of remorseless blizzards,
and — as though that were not enough — befouled with
the fumes and crushed with the weight of a thousand
loathsome cities, which are swift as the mushroom in
their growth, far more deadly than the *fungus fatalis* of
the Midi — it was here, passing with easy nonchalance
as the foal passes from one pasture to another, with a
flight swifter than the falcon's, luxurious in its appurte-
nance as a Shah's seraglio; it was here, in these whirling
circles of intrigue and pleasure and romance, and in this
span of an illimitable nomady, that flew the nights and
days of Philip, nineteenth Marquis of Vaulerois, as the
world knew him — " Fifi " of the First Life.

I am glad that in her later books Ouida has not de-
serted "the First Life." She is still the same Ouida,
has lost none of her romance, none of her wit and
poetry, her ebullitions of pity and indignation. The
old " naughtiness " and irresponsibility which were so
strange a portent in the Medio-Victorian days, and kept
her books away from the drawing-room table, seem to
have almost disappeared; and, in complement of her love

of luxury for its own sake, there is some social philosophy, diatribes against society for its vulgar usage of luxury. But, though she has become a mentor, she is still Ouida, still that unique, flamboyant lady, one of the miracles of modern literature. After all these years, she is still young and swift and strong, towering head and shoulders over all the other women (and all but one or two of the men) who are writing English novels. That the reviewers have tardily trumpeted her is amusing, but no cause for congratulation. I have watched their attitude rather closely. They have the idiot's cunning and seek to explain their behaviour by saying that Ouida has entirely changed. Save in the slight respect I have noted, Ouida has not changed at all. She is still Ouida. That is the high compliment I would pay her.

THE BLIGHT ON THE MUSIC HALLS

O Love! When you 're in love —
Love makes a man
Feel awf'lly peculiar.
O Love! When you 're in love —
With a Jane or a Julia,
Man falls in love!

These words, and their music, not less exquisite,
I owe to the erudition of a certain painter, who seems to
have spent most of the evenings of his life in Music Halls
and can bring forth from the storehouse of his memory many fatuous, forgotten choruses. Through the old
"Oxford" these words resounded from the great throat
of George Leybourne, nightly, years ago. Now they are
not remembered. They buzz no longer in brains that
are fulfilled with later melodies; and save, haply, in a far
county, by an old farmer, whose quiet life has not expunged

the memory of his visit to the town, you do nowhere hear
them carolled.   I am glad to resuscitate their rhythm :
bugle-notes to wake sleeping memories in some breasts ;
more melancholy for me, fainter, than scent of soever long-
kept lavender.

They belong to the unregenerate period of the Music
Halls.   In sense and sentiment and syntax, they differ
vastly from anything that one hears now.   Yet, in their
day, they were vastly popular, were typical, indeed, of all
the songs sung in the old " Oxford " or the " Albert "
or the " Hoxton Palace of Varieties."   To that sea of
billicocks, the audience, through that fog of cheap tobacco-
smoke, with the glare of footlights cast up on to his crum-
pled shirt-front and making a dark cavern of his mouth, the
Lion Comique bawled out always some such crude, conventional ditty.   And, when his turn was done, and he
had swaggered off that stage whose back-cloth was ever a
green glade with a portico or two of white marble, on
tripped his sister-artist, the badly-rouged Serio, gaudy in
satinette, energetic, hoarse, and without any talent.   Young
or old she might be, gracious or uncomely, might trip off,
at last, *non sine pastoricia fistula* or in a storm of approval
— what matter ?   She was ever the same Serio.   The convention was never broken.

Well ! I know these things only by tradition. If I fare to the Transpontine Halls, I find but an embarrassed remnant of the old performers, striving to live up to the imitators of Chevalier and Marie Lloyd. Reason, variety, refinement have crept gradually in, till one shall sigh in vain for the fatuous and delightful days of

> *Oh the Fairies ! Oh the Fairies !*
> *They are so tender,*
> *The feminine gender !*
> *Oh the Fairies ! Oh the Fairies !*
> *Oh for the wings of a Fairy Queen !*

But one must not marvel that those days are over. With sumptuous palaces erected in the heart of London, and with the patronage of fashion, new modes were bound to come in, sooner or later. The homely humour of James Fawn and Bessie Belwood was superseded, ere long, by Chevalier, with his new and romantic method; by Gus Elen, with his realistic psychology and his admirably written songs; by Marie Lloyd, with her swift *nuances*. Meanwhile — a new art ! Every one was interested. Every one had seen Mr. Sickert's paintings. Soon other painters began to frequent the Halls. Mr. Arthur Symons cut in, and secured the Laureateship. Mr. Anstey wrote

satires. Mr. Frederic Wedmore began to join in the
choruses with genteel gusto. And now, when, forwearied
with the demands of an intellectual life, I stray into the
Tivoli, and would fain soothe my nerves with folly, I find
an entertainment that is not only worthy of attention, but
is even most exigent of all my æsthetic faculties. There
is a swift succession of strongly, variously defined person-
alities, all trained and talented and self-conscious ; all in
pretty or appropriately grotesque costumes ; all imitating
this or that phase of modern life within the limits of their
new art. The words of their songs are quite pregnant
with character and wit. The music to which they are set
is no longer the eternal variation on one or two themes, but
is often novel and always adapted to the words' meaning.
When fatuousness and vulgarity take their turn, themselves
are in the nature of a surprise, startling, not soothing. I
find no repose for my faculties in the Tivoli. The atmosphere from the stage of it is surcharged with artistic
conscience. One knows that every performer is, in private life, a charming and serious person, whose photograph
is reproduced in the illustrated papers, from time to time,
with a description of his domestic life and his valuable
collection of proof-engravings, press-cuttings, and what not.
The interviewers have told one that he has a grand piano

in his drawing-room and often composes his own songs, and "will sing no words that he could not individually express." And one compares him, as he stands there, with that humble creature who sang, with very great success, years ago,

> *Then say was he a coward?*
> *Had he a coward's heart?*
> *By acting in this manner, did*
> *He play the coward's part?*
> *It was his earnest wish*
> *One day nobly to behave —*
> *And he proved himself at last to be*
> *The Bravest of the Brave.*

Does one, as I do, wish only for relaxation in Music Halls, he must needs go to Paris. There the Music Halls have been always kept in their proper perspective. Yvette Guilbert is but an accident. She was never *du Café Chantant*, and I hope she will soon retire to the legitimate stage. It is creditable to the Parisians that, despite her talent and individuality, she never found an imitatress. She was, indeed, the one jarring note in the *Ambassadeurs*, where, in a pale-green avenue, brilliant with white lights, one sought the restfulness of a fatuous convention; sought to be lulled by the eternal fat men, telling of *La Patrie* or of their *amouretts*, and by the voiceless, sprightly baggages, who sing eulogies of *Les Militaires*. Part of their charm for me is that, unless I listen, I know not what they are saying in their alien tongue. But they caper and gesticulate gracefully, and the light, familiar music soothes me   I have often thought that a man might end his days very pleasantly in the *claque*.

Between the French and the old English convention there are several points of difference, but each is based upon a monotonous vulgarity. Perhaps some person, who understands the charm of monotony, will say that in time our Music Halls will reach a plane of monotonous refinement, and that all will then be well. All would then be better, doubtless. But we have already the Italian Opera, and we have the Albert Hall. I insist that vulgarity is an implicit element of the true Music Hall. Why should we have sought to eliminate it? Out of the vulgarity of the people did the Music Hall arise, nor will any one be so foolish as to contend that, by tampering with its foundations, we shall go one step towards refining the people. In its early state, the Music Hall was a very curious and interesting phenomenon, a popular art. What better outlet for the people's vulgarity ? For cultured persons, what better κάθαρσις of that laughing and contemptuous spirit, which Aristotle knew to be a danger ? Vulgarity will, of course, last till the next Glacial Epoch, and we shall always be able to contemplate it. But we were fools to drive it from its most convenient haunt. Oh, for the wasted glories of the old Oxford ! Oh, for one hour in the Hoxton Palace of Varieties ! I must be glad that a few fragments have been snatched for me from their irrepleviable ditties. And, for my part, I do rejoice, in Summer and in Spring, in Autumn and in Winter, this sweet refrain to sing : —

> *He's a de-ar old pal of mine,*
> *He helped me when I was down,*
> *Lent me his aid,*
> *Willingly,*
> *With a smile, not a frown.*
> *And if the day should come,*
> *And my lucky star should shine,*
> *I shall always be*
> *Most happy to say*
> *" He's a de-ar old pal of mine ! "*

PRANGLEY VALLEY[1]

[1] *They who, having read pages 81–92, think that I ought to be Ædile, are earnestly requested not to read the beginning or the end of this essay. — M. B.*

"All men kill the thing they love" was the keynote of a fine ballad which every one has read. And, indeed, it does seem that in all love, be it love for animate or inanimate things, there is an ogre-ish element; humanity, in its egoism, being unable to appreciate anything, unless it have also power to destroy it. The comparative indifference with which the ancients regarded landscape might be traced to their lack of tools for its destruction. We, in this century, suffer from no such lack, and our love of landscape is quite unbounded. We have water-towers wherewith to cap our little hills, railway-trains to send along the ridges of our valleys, coal-shafts to sink through ground where, for many centuries, forests have been growing. We have factories, too, for the marges of wide rivers, texts about pills and soaps for the enamelling of meads, and telegraph-wires for the threading of air, and tall, black chimneys for all horizons. Month in, month out, with tears blinding our eyes, we raise tombs of brick and mortar for the decent burial of any scenery that may still be lying exposed. A little while, and English landscape will have become the theme of antiquarians, and we shall be listening to learned lectures on scenology and gaping at dried specimens of the trees, grasses, and curious flowers that were once quite common in our Counties.

I am glad that there are, in the meantime, still some fragments of country not built over. I make the most of them, whenever I am at leisure. I think that Prangley Valley is the fragment that most fascinates me ; partly because it is so utterly sequestered, yet so near to London. From Kew Gardens one may reach it in less than half an hour's walking, but the way to it lies through such devious and narrow lanes, that the wheel of no scorcher scars it, and it is unimpressed by any Arrian or Arriettian boot. Indeed, I have often wondered how the "King's Sceptre," a Jacobean inn which stands just above the Valley, can thrive so finely on so little custom. John Willet himself seemed not more prosperously-paunched than the keeper of this inn, and, though I have never met any fellow-farer at his door, my advent does not seem to flutter him. The notion that any human creature should care to drink old ale from one of his burnished tankards, or should admire the Valley over which he has always lived, seems to puzzle him rather, but not to excite him. It is very pleasant to sit on the settle that stands, in summer-time, across the lawn of his sloping garden; pleasant to sit there, among the hollyhocks and fuchsia-beds, and look down upon the little, hollow Valley that is so perfect in its way. I am afraid it is not a grand or an uncomfortable piece of scenery. It cannot lay claim to a single crag, peak, or torrent. It suggests the artfulness, rather than the forces, of Nature. Its charm is toy-like. The stream that duly bisects it is so slight and unassuming that I have quite forgotten its name. I remember that my innkeeper once told me, with a touch of pride, that it was a tributary of the Thames. Perhaps it is, but it looks suspiciously like a riband. So neat, so nicely matched one to another, are the poplar-trees on the opposite brow of the Valley, that one fancies they must stand, as in the nursery, on rounds of yellow wood, and would topple at the touch. Among these amusing trees there is one solitary tenement. It is a kind of pavilion, built of grey stone and crowned with a dome round which stand gilded statuettes of the nine Muses. I know not what happens in it now, but it is said to have been designed by Sir Roland Hanning, physician-in-ordinary to Queen Adelaide, and used by him as a summer-house and library, whenever he was in residence at Kew. Seen from a distance, with the sun gleaming on its grey and gilt, the pavilion has an absurd charm of its own. Set just where it is, it makes, in draughtsman's jargon, a pretty "spot" in the whole scheme. One can hardly believe, though, that any one but a marionette ever lived there. Indeed, were it not for the sheep, which are browsing on the slope and are obviously real, and for their shepherd, who is not at all like Noah, one would imagine that the whole Valley was but a large, expensive toy. A trim, demure prospect, unambitious, unspoilt! The strange brightness of its verdure and the correctness of its miniature proportions make it seem, in the best sense of the word, artificial. If it has not been designed and executed with intense care, it is certainly the luckiest of flukes. Greater it might be, but not better. I feel that, for what it is, it is quite perfect. So it soothes me, and I am fond of it.

I am not a railway-company, nor a builder, nor a County Councillor. I had no direct means of ruining Prangley Valley. But I have written my encomium of it, and now it is likely to be infested by all the readers of this book and by most of their friends. I have given away my poor Valley. The prospector will soon be prospecting it, and across its dear turf the trippers will soon be tripping. In sheer wantonness, I have ruined my poor Valley. Certainly, all true love has its ogre-ish element.

ARISE, SIR —— ——!

Knighthood is a cheap commodity in these days. It is modern Royalty's substitute for largesse, and it is scattered broadcast. Though all sneer at it, there are few whose hands would not gladly grasp the dingy patent. After all, a title is still a title. The provincial Mayor delights to think that, into whatsoever house he enter, his name will be announced with the very same prefix as would be the name of the best-emblazoned baronet, and that his wife will be as good, colloquially, as a Marchioness. Even now, the number of those who are not knighted exceeds the number of those who are. Time, doubtless, will reverse these figures. It is quite possible that, in the next century, forms of application for knighthood will be sent out annually to every householder and be thrown with other circulars into the wastepaper basket. Further still in the future, knighthood may

137

be one of the lighter punishments of the Law. " Forty shillings or a knighthood " sounds quite possible.

At present, there is no class more covetous of knighthood than that new class of writers which has come in on the wave of popular education. Well! they are an interesting class, these writers, and I should like them to be officially recognised. They are an honest, harmless crew, and I, for one, should like to see them made happy. By all means let them be knighted and their craft be stamped as a Profession. When Sir Walter Besant prattles to the fair readers of *The Queen* about the recognition of Literature as a Profession, he does not, of course, talk what is called sense; but these writers, whom I have named, have nothing to do with Literature — they are simply the first instalment of those who will supply a new commercial demand by giving the mob such stuff as it can appreciate. Writing, as practised by them, is at any rate a Trade, though no one save Sir Walter would call it a Profession. Mr. Flimflam, the popular novelist, is frankly of the moment, and, when he dies, another will take his place and will supply the same kind of stuff, with such variations as the superficial changes of the market may require. Being a man of average intelligence, he fully realises his transient position. He has no illusion that his works will outlive him, and his only hope is that they may continue to sell well up to the date of his death. He is in much the same position as is a great singer, who has to live his immortality in his life-time : he must needs make up in expansion what he cannot hope for in extent. Nor, indeed, is he coy of the necessity. He pushes his joints all round the market-place and basks in every available search-light. Some hours of the day he is bound to consecrate to his private life, in which, however, he keeps his readers very well posted, lest they forget, lest they forget. Probably, as the necessity for advertisement increases with the number of his rivals, he will have his house entirely rebuilt by a glazier, or he will pitch his writing-table in Trafalgar Square and sleep on the Embankment. But even now his must be a sadly arduous life. He must be the guest of the evening at the Inkslingers' Annual Dinner in the Holborn Restaurant, and there he must make an impromptu speech full of quaintly characteristic sayings. He must be the observed of all observers at the soirée given by the Institute of Second-Rate Lady-Journalists, and be seen at Private Views, bronzed and vigorous after his recent cruise on the Norfolk Broads. He must supply one of the most attractive items at the Concert in aid of the "Gunners' Orphanage" by giving a reading of two chapters from his military novel, *The Fifty-Second* (fiftieth thousandth), and be the victim of what might have proved a serious cab-accident, while he is being driven to the studio of Mr. Botch, R. A., who is painting him seated at a writing-table in the uniform of the North-Wilts Yeomanry (of which the popular author is an honorary captain). No one must know of the thousand-and-one little acts of delicate generosity with which Mr. Flimflam, not letting his right hand know what his left doeth, alleviates the lot of those old schoolmates who have been less successful than he in the struggle for life. After his lecturing-tour though the States, he must be off either to Venice, of which he is very fond, for a well-earned rest, or to Stoke Pogis, in order that he may put the finishing touches to his new mediæval novel, in which (it is an open secret) the love of Dante for Beatrice will be treated in a new and startling manner, though with all that reverence and wealth of local colour for which Mr. Flimflam's name is guarantee. Interviewed (or his name is not Flimflam) he must perpetually be, and for every interview he must be specially photographed with his favourite pipe, or with his cat and dog — Mr. Flimflam is a great lover of animals — or playing parlour-golf with

his only child, or riding on a " sociable " with his wife,
a charming brunette, very proud of her lord and master.
It must be known that he does a bit of gardening, now
and again, "just to brush away the cobwebs," and that
he laughingly confesses to being something of a philatelist.
A far-away look must come into his eyes — those grey,
deep-set eyes ! — as, slowly, quietly, he tells the interviewer the story of his early struggles in the old, old
days. The twilight must come creeping slowly into the
little room ; the needle-work must fall from Mrs. Flimflam's hands, as she too becomes absorbed in the oft-told
tale. At length, Mr. Flimflam must say, almost abruptly,
" But all that's over now ! Come ! You have yet to
see my bits of old oak. Yes, oak is quite a hobby with
me. My wife here tells me I ought to have been a
Druid ! '' Before the interviewer is sent on his way,
with a cordial handshake and a hope that he will return,
it must have been elicited that Mr. Flimflam has contracts
which will keep him at work well into the twentieth
century, and that in politics he is a Radical, though a
firm believer in the future of our Colonies, but that, as to
entering Parliament, that is not in his life-program —
" at least," he may add significantly, " not yet awhile !''
Poor fellow ! Why should he not receive his heart's

desire ?   What shoulders are more appropriate than Mr. Flimflam's to the touch of the royal sword ?   Disappointment may embitter him, and, if he were to be bitter, what would become of his books ?   If, on the other hand, his Sovereign summon him, I shall be at Paddington when, with elastic tread and boundless smile, he passes down the platform to the Windsor train.   It will do my heart good to see him.   For my own part, I should like him to have a life-peerage.   We have our Law-Lords — why not our Novel-Lords ?   It matters not what title he receive, so it be one which will perish, like his twaddle, with him.

FASHION AND HER BICYCLE

She still bestrides it, but how listlessly! A
little while, and she will suffer it to be wheeled into
that *musée sentimentale* wherein she keeps, duly classified,
specimens of her past foibles.

Let us tarry over the section there devoted to her foibles in the Victorian Era! There is the sketch-book,
whose leaves she did bedabble with timid water-colour, in
the 'forties, and the score of Bellini's *Ah! Non Giunge!*
and Donizetti's *O! Luce di quest Anima!* which she
did so wildly warble at the grand piano. Here are "the
gold arrow and the silver, the gold star and the silver,"
her guerdon in archery; there the gay mallet that sent
her ball so deftly through the iron hoops to the peg;
there the cameo she won in the Spelling Bee. Fond
memories of rinking lie in that pair of roller-skates, of
many hard-fought "sets," in that narrow, curved racquet.

10   145

This is a piece of " crewel-work : " note the silken in-
scription, *Five O' Clock Tea*, and the little figures at each
corner, copied from the " quaint " pages of Kate Green-
away. These are the fragments of a terra-cotta pigeon,
shot by Fashion, soon after she had " lived up to " that
tea-pot of blue china. This plain mackintosh hid her
diamonds when she went slumming. That is the very
lorgnon through which she was wont to spy, from her
seat on My Lord's bench, prisoners at the Old Bailey or
at Assizes. Here is the skirt she danced in a few years
ago. This was her banjo. This was her rubicon-
bézique marker, recently added to the collection. This
was her golf-club. And that long space — what is going
to be exhibited there ? Her bicycle.

I conceive that Fashion, when she goes the round of
her museum, will not tarnish this wheel with any tear.
How should she ? Craving some violent remedy for her
ennui, she sought to emulate St. Catharine. She suffered,
and flinched not. But, having once released herself, she
will not, I think, even when her bruises shall have faded
and her arm be unslung, wax fondly sentimental over the
wheel of her long agony. She will remember it only as
a horrid penance. Already she has dropped it from her
conversation ; Rudge, Humber, Singer — she cares no

longer to discriminate between machines which are, one and all of them, the devil's own patent. Indeed, she thinks, bicycling was ever the most tedious topic of conversation. It was also the most tedious form of exercise, save walking, known to the human race. It was but a strange, ingenious compound of dulness and danger. On a horse, Fashion would not mind risking her life, but there is a vast difference between a mount that is live and lovable and a mount that is manufactured of even the best steel. The one has fine qualities to be quickened, and swift caprices to be curbed, and is petulant or amenable, timid or too greatly daring, a thing of infinite surprises. The other has but one invariable motion, to whatsoever speed you may choose to regulate it. So soon as you can ride it, you have mastered all its charm, and, unless you be a professional acrobat, you can teach it nothing. It kills some of its riders, and bores the rest. I do not wonder that Fashion will have no more of it. Possibly, in the mellow haze of retrospect, she may forgive it its dulness and its danger. But there is one sin which she will never forgive it. It made her ugly and ridiculous. On it, for all the devices of her *coutourier*, Fashion never looked aught but her worst. In pursuit of her other foibles, at least she had always managed to look nice.

On the archery-lawn, gazing so seriously at "the gold," as she drew back her bow-string, paused, and let fly her arrow ; rinking, with her hands in a big muff and her fur cap tilted on the steep incline of her *chevelure ;* at croquet, daintily imposing a Balmoral-booted foot on the ball ; languorous in "utter" draperies among the peacock-feathers of 1880 ; or as she wheeled and darted hither and thither over the tennis-court, or as she sat, with bowed head, plucking the strings of her banjo, — in such attitudes as these, she was always a thing of gracious and delicate appeal. Perched to pedal the treadles, she was an effort, an anomaly, a fright.

I wish that Fashion's neglect could doom the bicycle. Of course, it cannot. The bicycle, long before it became Fashion's foible, had all the makings of a national institution, and Fashion's patronage has but speeded its triumphal progress through England. Some things were created by Fashion herself, and perished so soon as she was weary of them. Others, merely adopted by her, are more abiding. Golf, for example, as the most perfect expression of national stupidity, has an assured, uncheckered future, and croquet, as the one out-door game at which people can cheat, will never be in prolonged abeyance, and bicycling, as a symptom of that locomotomania produced by usage of steam, will endure " till we go back to the old coaches." The bicycle is complementary to the steam-engine, doing for the horseless individual what the steam-engine does for the community. It was as inevitable as it is unlovely, and I must put up with it. For the proletariat, it is not merely a necessity, but a great luxury, too. It gratifies that instinct which is common to all stupid people, the instinct to potter with machinery. In the hours of his leisure, if he be not riding, the cyclist is oiling his machine, or cleaning it when it is quite clean, or letting the air out of it for the simple pleasure of inflating it, or unscrewing it, or turning it upside down, or tapping it suspiciously with a pair of pincers. The sight of him is instructive. A mother's solicitude is not more tender than his. Observe him !

But, though the bicycle is a serious fact, and though Demos, with humped back and all the muscles of his face beetled down to one expression of grotesque and ghastly resolve, will continue to scorch through those clouds of dust which mercifully obscure his outlines or those baths of mud which he would have me share with him, yet I may bid a glad farewell to the bicycle as Fashion's foible. To Fashion, the bicycle was but a new toy, not a necessity. The dame is rich, and can afford horses, and her horses will be a proud symbol of her superiority, hereafter as in the past. Next century, she will tower equestrian in the bikish chaos, and the horses of her barouche will shy among the serried motor-cars of the middle-class. For the moment, my chief curiosity is of her next foible. Motor-cars, even as toys, seem not to enrapture her. For the flying-machine she may have yet to wait. *En attendant?* There are many things for her selection. The concertina is a rather nice instrument. Stilts are not to be despised. Mohammedanism is said to be fascinating, and so are tip-cat and the tight-rope.

GOING BACK TO SCHOOL

The other evening, at about seven o'clock, I was in a swift hansom. My hat was tilted at a gay angle, and, for all I was muffled closely, my gloves betokened a ceremonious attire. I was smoking *la cigarette d'appetit,* and was quite happy. Outside Victoria my cab was stopped by a file of other cabs, that were following one another in at the main entrance of the station. I noticed, on one of them, a small hat-box, a newish trunk and a corded play-box, and I caught one glimpse of a very small, pale boy in a billicock-hat. He was looking at me through the side-window. If Envy was ever inscribed on any face, it was inscribed on the face of that very small, pale boy. "There," I murmured, "but for the grace of God, goes Max Beerbohm!"

My first thought, then, was for myself. I could not but plume me on the contrast of my own state with

153

his. But, gradually, I became fulfilled with a very great compassion for him. I understood the boy's Envy so well. It was always the most bitter thing, in my own drive to the station, to see other people, quite happy, as it seemed, with no upheaval of their lives ; people in cabs, who were going out to dinner and would sleep in London ; grown-up people ! Than the impotent despair of those drives — I had exactly fifteen of them — I hope that I shall never experience a more awful emotion. Those drives have something, surely, akin with drowning. In their course the whole of a boy's home-life passes before his eyes, every phase of it standing out against the black curtain of his future. The author of *Vice-Versa* has well analyzed the feeling, and he is right, I think, in saying that all boys, of whatsoever temperament, are preys to it. Well do I remember how, on the last day of the holidays, I used always to rise early, and think that I had got twelve more whole hours of happiness, and how those hours used to pass me with mercifully slow feet. . . . Three more hours ! . . . Sixty more minutes ! . . . Five ! . . . I used to draw upon my tips for a first-class ticket, that I might not be plunged suddenly among my companions, with their hectic and hollow mirth, their dreary disinterment of last term's

154

jokes. I used to revel in the thought that there were many stations before G———. . . . The dreary walk, with my small bag, up the hill ! I was not one of those who made a rush for the few cabs . . . The awful geniality of the House Master ! The jugs in the dormitory ! . . . Next morning, the bell that woke me ! The awakening !

Not that I had any special reason for hating school ! Strange as it may seem to my readers, I was not un-popular there. I was a modest, good-humoured boy. It is Oxford that has made me insufferable. At school, my character remained in a state of undevelopment. I had a few misgivings, perhaps. In some respects, I was always too young, in others, too old, for a perfect relish of the convention. As I hovered, in grey knickerbockers, on a cold and muddy field, round the outskirts of a crowd that was tearing itself limb from limb for the sake of a leathern bladder, I would often wish for a nice, warm room and a good game of hunt-the-slipper. And, when we sallied forth, after dark, in the frost, to the swimming-bath, my heart would steal back to the fireside in Writing School and the plot of Miss Braddon's latest novel. Often, since, have I wondered whether a Spartan system be really well for youths who are bound mostly for

Capuan Universities. It is true, certainly, that this system makes Oxford or Cambridge doubly delectable. Undergraduates owe their happiness chiefly to the consciousness that they are no longer at school. The nonsense which was knocked out of them at school is all put gently back at Oxford or Cambridge. And the discipline to which they are subject is so slight that it does but serve to accentuate their real freedom. The sudden reaction is rather dangerous, I think, to many of them.

Even now, much of my own complacency comes of having left school. Such an apparition as that boy in the hansom makes me realise my state more absolutely. Why, after all, should I lavish my pity on him and his sorrows? *Dabit deus his quoque finem.* I am at a happier point in Nature's cycle. That is all. I have suffered every one of his ordeals, and I do not hesitate to assure him, if he chance to see this essay of mine, how glad I am that I do not happen to be his contemporary. I have no construe of Xenophon to prepare for to-morrow morning, nor any ode of Horace to learn, painfully, by heart. I assure him that I have no wish nor any need to master, as he has, at this moment, the intricate absurdities of that proposition in the second book of Euclid. I have no locker, with my surname printed on it and a complement

of tattered school-books. I burnt all my school-books,
when I went up to Oxford. Were I to meet, now, any
one of those masters who are monsters to you, my boy,
he would treat me even more urbanely, it may be, than
I should treat him. When he sets you a hundred lines,
you write them without pleasure, and he tears them up.
When I, with considerable enjoyment and at my own
leisure, write a hundred lines or so, they are printed for
all the world to admire, and I am paid for them enough
to keep you in pocket-money for many terms. I write
at a comfortable table, by a warm fire, and occupy an
arm-chair, whilst you are sitting on a narrow form. My
boots are not made "for school-wear," nor do they ever,
like yours, get lost in a litter of other boots in a cold
boot-room. In a word, I enjoy myself immensely. To-
night, I am going to a theatre. Afterwards, I shall sup
somewhere and drink wine. When I come home and
go to bed, I shall read myself to sleep with some amusing
book. . . . You will have torn yourself from your bed,
at the sound of a harsh bell, have washed, quickly, in
very cold water, have scurried off to Chapel, gone to first
school and been sent down several places in your form,
tried to master your next construe, in the interval of
snatching a tepid breakfast, been kicked by a bigger boy,

and had a mint of horrible experiences, long before I, your elder by a few years, have awakened, very gradually, to the tap of knuckles on the panel of my bedroom-door. I shall make a leisurely toilet. I shall descend to a warm breakfast, open one of the little budgets which my "damned good-natured friend," Romeike, is always sending me, and glance at that morning paper which appeals most surely to my sense of humour. And when I have eaten well of all the dishes on the table, I shall light a cigarette. Through the haze of its fragrant smoke, I shall think of the happy day that is before me.

"A. B."

Every week, I am fain of certain serious and comic papers, solely for the sake of Mr. Alfred Bryan's drawings. Some of these papers are obscure, others are tedious, but, in that "A. B." irradiates each one of them, I never miss *Judy*, *The Entr' Acte*, *Moonshine*, *The Sporting and Dramatic Times*, and *Ally Sloper's Half Holiday*. Altogether, I owe a rather heavy debt of gratitude to Mr. Alfred Bryan. Statistics are not, perhaps, a very high form of art-criticism, but I cannot help calculating, in an idle moment, that I see, every year, more than eleven hundred new examples of Mr. Bryan's work. None of that work is exquisite, as I need hardly say. It is but a monstrous profusion of odd jobs, including portraits, caricatures, political cartoons, studies in character, views of banquets or race meetings, theatrical cartoons, advertisements, illustrations, and a vast number of other things. Omnicipient in material, the master of many styles, Mr. Bryan never trips nor blunders, and is always absolutely himself.

In these days of feverish questing, when not to have discovered at least one new genius every month is as much as an art critic's place is worth, how comes it that Mr. Bryan still waits for his discovery ? There is more talent in his little finger than in half the emblazoned hierarchy of "pen-and-ink draughtsmen," on whose potterings and peddlings we all lavish so much admiration. Except Mr. Phil May and Mr. Raven Hill, there is no one, engaged in pen-and-ink work of a popular kind, who can be compared with him, merely in point of technical mastery. How comes it that the critics neglect him? Our journals are packed with praise of Mr. Phil May, with dissertations on his "line" and his "economy of means," and his "Dickens-like knowledge of, and sympathy with, the lower classes." We never tire of reading that, in private life, he is the prince of good fellows, and has an observant twinkle in his eye, and does innumerable studies for his slightest drawings. None admits gladlier than I the brilliancy of his work. I was, indeed, one of his first admirers. Fourteen years ago, at a very tender age, I "discovered" him in the *St. Stephen's Review*, and was very sorry when he ceased to draw for that paper. I know, moreover, that he has a most interesting personality, and that his life has been full of changes and of adventures, nor do I grudge the journalists their copy. Of Mr. Bryan's personality I know nothing at all. Perhaps he is quite colourless. But I cannot, for the life of me, see that his work is less remarkable than Mr. Phil May's. I admit that an average drawing of Mr. May's is artistically more valuable than an average drawing of Mr. Bryan's. Mr. May is always doing his best, Mr. Bryan is not. Mr. May walks around, observes life, ruminates on it, selects some phases of it, looks out for suitable models, does his innumerable studies, and, finally, after a long process of rejection, produces a drawing. There is no "beastly pride" about Mr. Alfred Bryan. He would seem to be always scudding up and down for immediate material, tearing home, clutching at a pen and dashing off the requisite number of drawings of the requisite kind — with a good riddance to the printer's devil at the door. Under such conditions, he cannot do his best, naturally. But Mr. Bryan at his worst is quite wonderful. He has an absolute knowledge of his craft, the very surest of hands. If he

scamped all his drawings, they would be admirable. Indeed, his spontaneity is one of his greatest charms. I
would willingly sacrifice the whole life-work of certain
honoured draughtsmen for one of those astounding things
in *The Entr' Acte*.

It has still to be asked why the British Public has not
pressed Mr. Bryan, as it has pressed (say) Mr. F. C.
Gould, to its Great Heart. Mr. Gould was certainly
not placed there by the art critics, for, so far from taking
that care of his *technique*, which does always impress
them, he has no *technique* to take care of. His drawings
are quite crude, quite flat, and, save as the designs of a
clever partisan, quite worthless. Yet there he is! And
there he came, if I am not mistaken, through his own
shrewdness. He specialised. His signature was soon
associated with one journal and with one kind of cartoon.
Last General Election raised his work to the level of a
party-question and crystallised his fame. If one wish for
further proof that a narrow range is commercially helpful,
let him consider the dullard draughtsman, who produces,
week after week, his race-horse or bicycle-girl or ballet-
dancer or whatever-his-fake-may-be. But for his obses-
sion, would this genius ever have become popular ? It is
Mr. Bryan's misfortune — and his charm and strength,

also — that he has never specialised. He deals with
everything and modulates his style for every subject. All
artists, I know, pass through certain phases of style in the
course of their lives, but Mr. Bryan keeps his various
phases always ready, all the week round, docketed (as
who should say) or on tap. He does caricatures for
The Entr' Acte, and though he is not malign enough to
be a caricaturist by bent, his caricatures are the best I
ever see, simple, swift, and slap-dash, *pro natura generis*.
He does innumerable portraits, some slight, others elaborate, of all great and little celebrities, and I think that, in
the trick of "catching a likeness," he has no rival. His
portraits have not the psychological value of Mr. Leslie
Ward's. "Spy" steeps himself in the tone and character of his subject, whilst Mr. Bryan cannot afford time
for that process. He gets his material solely from the
surface, from the bare lineaments, at a glance, and,
though he fails often in character, so sure is his eye that
he never fails to portray quite faithfully the most insipid
and "unseizable" creature. His cartoons, again, in
Moonshine, are not so impressive as Sir John Tenniel's,
though, doubtless, he would have been a knight ere now,
had he confined himself to cartoons. Nor have they so
much *connaissance de cause* as one finds in those of Mr. F.

C. Gould. But they are full of strength and humour and imagination. Alone, they would suffice for a great reputation. When, likewise, Mr. Bryan illustrates stories, his work might serve as a good example to the nincompoops of the monthly magazines, and he is positively able to get some effect out of those hideous " process-blocks." In fact, he is *capable de tout*. To his every undertaking, he brings a plastic, forcible style and a mastery of line. His most intricate pictures, filled with scores of figures, are all works of art, in their way, decorative and synthetic. You need but consider the work of his imitators (his only symptom of fame!) to see what a great artist he is. His profusion has blinded the eyes of the art-critics to his great merit. The art-critics judge him by one or two of his drawings, seen here or there, casually, and never do they suppose that he should be judged in the bulk of his work. His profusion has tired and glutted the public, which associates his name with nothing in particular. There is something sad in his profusion.

> *Not an eye*
> *But is awearied of his common sight,*
> *Save mine!*

For myself, I should be sorry to see him engaged exclusively by one newspaper, and should not care if he were to do even a greater number of drawings than he does now. I like the cool regularity with which he keeps his various styles ajob. The modern juggler, spinning his unbroken cycle of a top-hat, two gloves, a cigar, and a spread umbrella, is not more marvellous than he. Mr. Paul Cinquevalli may not have mastered all the possibilities of his cigar. He cannot, perhaps, exhale it through his eyelids or blow rings through his ears, as some more single-minded persons can do. And Mr. Alfred Bryan, likewise, may not have got all that is to be got out of any one of his styles. Yet, his whole performance does interest me more than Mr. Phil May's, more than that of any popular black-and-white artist, who does the best of his kind. Mr. Bryan himself is probably unconscious that his work is at all wonderful. He is content to work for the passing moment, content that his drawings all go to quick oblivion. But I must venture to discriminate for him. There is one section of his work so admirable and so unrivalled that it deserves to be remembered always. In his theatrical sketches, nobody, I think, can approach him, nor can any of my superlatives do them full justice. For how long he has done those weekly sketches in *The Sporting and Dramatic*, I am not quite certain, but I should put the period at sixteen years. Any one who has ever tried to draw actors or actresses from any part of the auditorium, or to get any positive and definite impression of those moving figures, will know how utterly hopeless the effort is. Mr. Bryan is sole master of the secret. His sketches of all the *dramatis personæ*, even of those who only appear on the stage for a few moments, are all miracles of acute observation and spontaneous humour. Week by week, they display his talent as its very best, its swiftest and most plastic. One finds in them examples of all his many styles, of all his inventiveness. An anthology of them would be a nice tribute to Mr. Bryan's genius. It would be, also, an interesting record of the modern English stage. It ought to be made.

A CLOUD OF PINAFORES

The modish appanage of Beauty in her barouche is not a spaniel, now, but a little child. The wooden wicket which, even in my day, barred the topmost of the stairs, has been taken off its hinges, and the Jewels roll down into Cornelia's drawing-room at will. Cornelia's callers are often privileged to a place at nursery-tea. The bread-and-butter is not cut thick, as in their day, and that old law, which made it precedent of cake, seems to have been rescinded. Nor is any curb set on little tongues. Cornelia and her callers grow glad in the frolic of artless *aperçus*. They are sick of *sèvres* and scandal. Only the fresh air of the nursery can brace their frail bodies and keep up their weary eyelids.

Yes! A casual optimist might proclaim that the Victorian Era is harking back to its first simplicity. At the risk of saddening him, I must suggest that he examine his opinion. I fear there are flaws in it. Between the Georgian and Victorian Eras came an interval of transition. Society was tired of its old pleasures, but did not quite abandon them. It still masked and gambled, but only a little, in a quiet way, as by force of habit. It was really resting. And when William died and was succeeded by a young Queen, herself a symbol of all simplicity, it was ready for renunciation. It had regained its old strength, was strong enough to be simple. In the gradual years, after the Queen-widow had withdrawn herself, ceding the supremacy to her eldest son, Society slipped into its old ways. Surfeit came in due course. Men and women sought refuge in bizarre fashions : æstheticism, slumming, Buddhism. But now surfeit has come again. They look around. What is left to them ? Simplicity ! But they are tired. There is no interval for rest. Also, they are less strong physically, intellectually stronger, than were their grandparents ; not strong enough, not weak enough, to be simple. But ah ! there is one thing left to them. They can, at least, contemplate simplicity. There is a nursery somewhere at the top of most houses. " Let the children be brought down to lunch ! Let us have tea with the children !"

One may trace, in the evolution of modern literature,

a fairly exact parallel. But the cross-lines which connect the corresponding points on either side of this parallel are uniformly oblique. It may be too much to say that Life always copies Literature, yet certainly Literature is always a little ahead of Life. Thus we find that Pre-Raphaelite poets were at work before 1880, that Sir Walter Besant, too, was already bustling about the slums, and Buddha peeping from many a first, second, and third volume. Nor did Stevenson write his *Child's Garden*, nor Pater his *Child in the House*, to meet a demand which was as yet uncreated ; nor, indeed, did either work attract any atten-. tion. But, now that children are booming, the publishers and the reviewers are all agog. Stevenson and Mr. Walter Crane are honoured with reprints. " Mr. Pater's most exquisite achievement is *The Child in the House* " — " *Sentimental Tommy* is the supreme outcome of Mr. Barrie's genius" — " Mr. Kenneth Grahame's *Golden Age* is indeed a Golden Book." Yes ! Children are in vogue. The clear carillon of the coral-and-bells has penetrated even to the back-benches of the Divorce Court, and the assiduous, unimportant authors, who sat scribbling there, have torn up their flimsies and scuttled forth at the summons. *Faut être dans le mouvement*, poor creatures ! For a while, they will make the scrap-screen their back-

ground. And if their heroine wear a pinafore, not a
strange tea-gown " of some clinging green material," and
prefer jam to laudanum and make-believe to introspection,
I, for one, shall see nothing lamentable in the difference.
Save as a guide to tendencies of the period, such writers
do not interest me much.

I find a far subtler and more amusing guide in a
little book entitled *The Children*, and written by a lady
whose talent is pre-eminently, almost painfully, adult.
Here, indeed, is a perfect example of our tecnolatry, our
delight in the undirected oddities of children, our wistful
effort to understand them as they are. We are told of a
boy who, at the sea-side, "assumes a deep, strong, and
ultra-masculine note, and a swagger in his walk, and gives
himself the name of his father's tallest friend. The tone
is not wholly manly ; it is a tone of affairs, and withal
careless ; it is intended to suggest business, and also the possession of a top-hat and a pipe, and is known in the family
as his 'official voice.' " How nicely sympathetic is this
analysis of a mood which, in my day, was called "show-
ing-off," and was invariably discouraged ! " 'Listen
to him, mother,' " says a little girl, " 'he's trying to
talk like God. He often does.' " In the unkind 'sixties
this little girl would have been sent to bed as a blas-

phemer. In my day, she would have been told that what she said was irreverent, and that irreverence was a very terrible thing. She " seemed thoroughly to understand the situation " is our author's comment. Indeed the modern feeling is that the child can do no wrong. Its very slips in grammar, its inconsequence, its confusion of names, are all treasured with a loving care and imbued with an exquisite significance. " A nut-brown child of five was persuading another to play. ' Oh come,' she said, ' and play with me at new maid.' " Formerly, no amount of nut-brownness would have saved her from an explanation that the game was called " old " maid ; as it is, I am quite sure she was kissed for her mistake by whatever grown-up person overheard it.

Certainly, I should be the last to deprecate the vogue of children, if I were to regard it from a selfish and superficial standpoint. For if there be one thing which people love more than to read about children, now, it is to read what children write. Had I not been *parmi les jeunissimes*, I should not have made the little success I have. The public does not, I suppose, care greatly whether I write well nor whether my premises and conclusions be correct. But it knows me to be a child-author, and likes to picture me at my desk, dressed in black velveteen,

175

with legs dangling towards the floor. If I filled this book
with the pot-hooks and hangers, which were, till recently,
my sole literary output, the public would be just as well
pleased. But, though this sparkling tide flows all in my
favour, I cannot quite approve of it. To me, there
seems some danger in the prevalent desire to observe
children in their quiddity, to leave them all to their
own devices and let them develop their own natures,
swiftly or slowly, at will. Perhaps I am bigoted and
old-fashioned, out of touch with the time. But I
must confess that, sometimes, my heart does even hark
back to those stern old Georgian or Early Victorian days,
when nurseries were governed in a spirit of blind despo-
tism. Children were not then recognised as human
creatures. They were a race apart ; savages that must
be driven from the gates ; beasts to be kept in cages ;
devils to whose voices one must not listen. Indeed, the
very nature of children was held to be sinful. Lies and
sloth, untidiness and irreverence, and a tendency to steal
black currant jam, were taken to be its chief constituents.
And so all nurseries, as one may learn from old books or
from the oral tradition, were the darkened scene of tem-
poral oppression, fitfully lighted with the gaunt reflections
of hell-fire. How strange a picture is to be found in

those books of "cautionary verses for children," irrele-
vantly entitled *The Daisy* and *The Cowslip*. Anything less flower-like than their tone could not be
easily conceived. The good children who move through
their pages are the merest puppets, worked by the monstrous autocrat, Mamma, whilst the bad children, placed
there as foils, are the most mechanical of drones and
dunces. Never once does the authoress betray the
briefest wish to treat children objectively. Yet, curious
though it seem to modern ideas, she typifies the parents
of her period.

Children were not neglected in those days. Their
parents' sedulous endeavour was to force them up to a
standard of mature conduct. They were taught that
only their elders were good, and they were punished
always in so far as they behaved childishly. See, even,
how they were dressed! Miss Caroline, when she
walked out, was framed in a crinoline, and she shaded her
ringlets with a minute parasol, whilst Master Richard,
her brother, in nankeen trousers, was a small replica of
his papa. Later, in the 'seventies and 'eighties, before
the Child, as such, was cared for, we see the little girl
still tricked out in the latest fashion of maturity, and the
little boy masquerading as a highlander or as a sailor.

Nowadays, they are both put into the limpest, simplest "things." The 'nineties wish children to be children, and nothing more. If— to take but one of the many pregnant comparisons suggested by *The Daisy* or *The Cowslip* — a little girl of this period be suffering toothache, she is coaxed, by all manner of sweet means, to the dentist's chair. Her fears could not anger any one. She is a child. But read the "cautionary verses" about two sisters, Miss Clara and Miss Sophie, who "both had faded teeth." Miss Clara, like a good grown-up lady, realised that a short wrench were as nothing to such prolonged agony. Miss Sophie held back, trembling. No one reasoned with her. She was suffered to be a foil to the adult fortitude of her sister, whose

> *teeth returned quite fresh and bright,*
> *Whilst Sophie's ached both day and night.*

These are a type of the verses that were written for children of the last generation, as *The Fairchild Family* is a type of the prose. Even in books like *Struwelpeter* the elements of terror were lurking everywhere. When children came into the scheme of a novel, they were, with few exceptions, prigs like Little Nell and Paul Dombey ; dreary abstractions, foredoomed to the earliest of death-

178

beds. In fact, real children were pariahs. That, you will say, was horrible and inhuman of their elders. It was. But I am inclined to think that, for the children themselves, it was a far more wholesome state of things. For the inherent nature of childhood is far brighter than the inherent nature of maturity. Childhood has no alien responsibilities, it is free from all the bitterness of knowledge and of memory, is careless and hopeful. So that, if the nursery be turned into a free republic and be rid of its old gloom and vigilant authority, it must be the scene of absolute happiness, and its children, when the time comes for them to leave it, will be appalled by the serious side of life. Finding no pleasure in a freedom which they have always had, incapable of that self-control which long discipline produces, they will become neurotic, ineffectual men and women. In the old days there could have been no reaction of this kind. The strange sense of freedom was a recompense for less happiness of heart. Children were fit for life.

Even from the standpoint of those elders, to whose jaded longing for simplicity the new form of education must be traced, there is great reason for misgiving. For it is probable that the effort to keep children simple by leaving them free, will but exterminate simplicity, at last. It is only oppression that can keep human beings as they are. Oppression never crushes natural instincts. All history proves that it does but intensify them. Wronged races are always primitive. Left to themselves, they develop. If Home Rule were granted, the Irish would soon lose their irresponsible gaiety, which centuries of oppression have preserved for them. Indeed, that is perhaps the most valid argument against Home Rule. Miss Caroline, likewise, and Master Richard, driven to bay by their elders, set their back against the nursery wall and were simple to the last. But Jock and Millicent, encouraged in all their childishness, having but their own natures to think of, will very soon become self-conscious. "Whenever I can't stop laughing I have only to think of home." These words were written by a little boy from his first boarding-school, and are quoted in *The Children*. So you see that introspection has set in already, and soon every high-chair will hold its lisping Rousseau or Marie Bashkirtseff. And soon there will be no more simplicity to contemplate. And what will a jaded world, straining at its tether, do then? Personally, I should like to think that this passion for simplicity was the sign of a lessening complexity. But wishes beget poor thoughts. I write what I believe to be true about this Victorian era. Good has been followed by evil, evil by the love of mysteries, the love of mysteries by the love of simple things. Observe that I write no fool's prattle about *le fin du siècle*. A phase of social evolution happens to coincide with a certain point in the kalendar. That, of course, is a mere chance. But we may be allowed to laugh, when we see that this century, for which Science promised a mature perfection, is vanishing in a white cloud of pinafores.

AT COVENT GARDEN

I am quite indifferent to serious music, and I should not suffer from any sense of loss if all the scores of all the operas that have ever been written, and all the persons who might be able to reconstruct them from memory, were to perish in a sudden holocaust to-morrow. And yet I like going to Covent Garden. In June and July it is not the least pleasant mode of whiling away the half-hour between dinner and supper. With its cool vestibules and colonnades and *foyers*, Covent Garden, despite its humble site and comparatively mean proportions, is an ideal place for a cigarette. Merely to wander behind the Grand Tier and read the illustrious names printed on the doors of the boxes — printed in mere black and white, just as my name will be printed on the label of this wretched book — is an experience to thrill hearts that are far less snobbishly impressionable than my heart is.

I seem to breathe, at every step I take in that circuit, the tart ozone of distinction. The sultriness of no night in summer can rob me of the exhilaration which fills my being in that most high and rarefied and buoyant atmosphere. I seem to tread the circuit with very light feet. Soon I am of a mood for the auditorium. As I pass down one of the narrow stairways leading to that sea of sleek heads and jewelled or feathered *coiffures*, the stalls, a stout gentleman unconsciously obstructs my path. As he makes way for me, I recognize in him, from an old drawing in *Punch*, an hereditary legislator who was once in one of Mr. Gladstone's Cabinets. *En passant*, I tread upon his foot, that I may have the honour of apologising to him. He bows courteously. I am happy. On the vast and cavernous stage, behind low-burning footlights, some opera or other is proceeding. The fiddlers are fiddling in a quiet monotone, not loud enough to drown the chatter in the stalls and boxes. All around me the people are chattering to one another like so many smart apes. Snatches of discussion here, and of flirtation there, are wafted past me, gaily, ceaselessly. I see the flash of eager gestures in white kid ; I see white shoulders, white gardenias, rouge under lurid œiliads, the quivering of *aigrettes*, the light on high collars highly-polished, and

186

the sheen of innumerable diamonds, and the rhythmic sway of a thousand-and-one fans. Row upon row, the little dull-red boxes, receptacles of bravery and beauty, are sparkling, also, with ceaseless animation. To me they are like an exquisite panorama of Punch-and-Judy shows. Every lady, I think, should bring her lap-dog and set it on the ledge of her box, to consummate the illusion. Just above me, to my right, stretches an omnibus-box. Olympian ! It is empty, save for one of whom nothing can be seen but a large *lorgnon* upheld by a pair of small, fat, tight-gloved hands. Who is it ? A great man, doubtless. Great ; else he were not hidden. A *virtuoso*, too ; else he were less rapt. Perhaps an Ambassador ; for his cuffs are cut in a foreign mode. Yes, I am sure those are the cuffs of an old diplomat, and that their wearer has sat, just so, hidden behind the curtain, in all the opera-houses of Europe — the Ring Theatre, the Théâtre de la Monnaie, the Hof Opern-Haus, La Scala, and the rest. So will he yet be sitting next year, here or in some other city.

And the music, the incidental music, is being played all this while. I do not think it is Wagner's. Wagner is usually rather obtrusive and apt to forget his place. He forgets the deference due to the stalls and boxes,

forcing their occupants to shout at the tops of their
voices if they would be heard, and has a vulgar trick of
playing to the Amphitheatre and its dowdy freight of lis-
teners. But he has done undeniably good work in hum-
bling the singers. Thanks to him, the audience no longer
spends its evening in prostration before a *prima donna*.
Bouquets do not hurtle through the air, and the poor singers,
with their diamonds, and their diet, and their rivalries, and
their *roulades*, are not the cynosure they were in the 'seventies. Yet, there they still are, those tiny, inadequate puppets on that mammoth-stage, mere dots like the human
figures on one of Turner's widest canvases ; here he still is,
this fat little man in trunk hose, with yellow hair down his
back, strutting, storming, spurning, suppliant, passionate,
aspiring, desperate — all for the sake of a little lady in
white, with her hands clasped across her breast and her
face upturned to the property stars. These little mario-
nettes with big voices, making so gigantic a pother about
something or other, have keen pathos in my sight — types
of our poor estate, of our vanity, our pompous endeavour-
ing, our insignificance, on the world's stage. See ! The
wee tenor is going to kill himself with a dagger. No !
The wee soprano prevents him. Tiny, intelligent, full
of purpose, performing with all their might tasks for

which I see no reason, they seem to me — these two —
like a pair of ants on a pathway :

> " *Hi motus animorum atque hæc certamina tanta*
> *Pulveris exigui jactu compressa quiescunt.*"

Hark ! They are in the midst of a stormy duet. I
vow the little creatures fascinate me ! Here comes a
whole army of ants in attitudes of surprise. The wee
tenor beats his breast, the wee soprano dashes down a
cup of wine. I would not throw dust on them for all
the world ! But some one, less kind than I, rolls down a
great curtain, and the ants are hidden. The audience
stops talking for a few moments of rather languid applause.
Men in the stalls stand up and stare around, sidle their
way through the crush in Fops' Alley, and seek the
Tiers. The Ambassador in the omnibus-box has dropped
his *lorgnon* and is quite invisible now. And I reflect
that, after all, the ants were rather absurd, and that,
really, the house is rather hot, and that, on the whole, I
will not stay for the last act.

THE CASE OF PROMETHEUS

Mr. Richard Mitchell, than whom no traveller is held to be more reliable and (if I may say so) more prosaic, returned to this country at the close of last year, after a long tour through Asiatic Russia. In the paper which he read lately before the Royal Geographical Society he reported a most curious and most important discovery. It seems that, in surveying the eastern side of Mount Caucasus, he espied through his telescope what appeared to be a naked figure on a rock near the mountain's summit. When he reached the little village of Tzeva in the valley, he told what he had seen to his innkeeper, who crossed himself repeatedly and was silent. Pressed by Mr. Mitchell to say if he knew anything of the figure, the man said that it must have been the *putchki velkotsin* (white captive) ; more he could not, or would not, communicate. Mr. Mitchell learnt from other peasants that the figure had been there for many years : indeed, they thought, ever since God made the world.   He offered money to any one who would make an ascent with him — it seemed hopeless, at that time of year, that any man could without help gain so high an altitude — but the peasants, one and all, refused his offer with every manifestation of superstitious awe.   Mr. Mitchell then decided that he would try the ascent alone, and, next day, he set forth.   He reached the spot whence he had first seen the figure, and, after trying various paths, managed at length to reach a point some three hundred feet below the summit.   Beyond this point the ground was utterly impassable.   "The sun was low in the west," says Mr. Mitchell, "but I could see clearly what was indeed a naked man chained by the wrists and ankles to an upstanding rock.   I noticed that his body was covered with scars, but at first I was not sure whether he was alive or dead.   I shouted and waved my knapsack in the air.   The captive turned his head in my direction, thus enabling me to get a full view of his face, which was that of a young man, though horribly drawn, emaciated, and rigid with exposure.   His hair hung down over his shoulders like a mantle, and it was weighted with long icicles.   I shouted again.   The cap-

tive uttered a faint moan.   I could see the tears stream
down his cheeks, freezing as they fell.   He seemed to be
trying to speak, but at that moment my attention was dis-
tracted to an enormous golden eagle — larger than any I
have ever seen — which had appeared in the sky and was
wheeling slowly over the summit.   In a few moments
the creature swooped suddenly down and began tearing
at the wretched man's body.   The sight sickened me so
that I had to turn my head away, cursing my impotence
to interfere.   When I looked again, the bird was already
soaring high in the air.   In the failing light I could see
that the captive had fainted and that blood was flowing
from a long wound in his side.''   Night was falling, and
after a desperate and fruitless effort to reach the summit,
Mr. Mitchell felt that he himself must either perish of
exposure or re-descend the mountain.   So agitated was
he by what had passed that it was some hours before he
realised, suddenly, that he had seen Prometheus.   At
Truoff, two days later, he communicated with the military governor of the province, whose only reply was to
send him with an escort across the frontier.

That this story is fiction, no one who knows Mr.
Mitchell's record could possibly aver.   That Mr. Mitchell
was a prey to one of those illusions which do sometimes

beset men on very high altitudes, is an equally unten-
able theory — as Mr. Mitchell himself said in the course
of his lecture, he is "an old mountaineer and had seen
nothing unusual on the Himalayas." The only question is whether the captive on the mountain is really (as
Mr. Mitchell declares, and as I myself am persuaded) to
be identified with Prometheus. It is known that Prometheus, by order of Jupiter, was chained to the summit
of this mountain ; that his punishment was to last for
thirty thousand years ; that on every day of all those years
he was to be preyed upon by Jupiter's own bird. So far,
so good. But Professor Thorsby, in a letter to the
Times, points out that Hercules is generally believed
to have rescued Prometheus thirty years after sentence
was passed. Now, this belief rests on very dubious
authority. In the works of Diodorus there is no reference to any such rescue, and Sidonius Strabo himself, in
the *Quaestiones Olympianae,* expressly states that no such
rescue occurred. At the very time when, according to
Hesiod, Hercules was seen in the region of Mount
Caucasus, he was actually in Central Lydia, a slave at
the court of Omphale, that frivolous Queen. And inas-
much as, during that period — and, indeed, during
the rest of his mortal life — he was expiating his sins

against the gods, and carefully qualifying for Olympus, it is in the highest degree improbable that he would have thrown away his chance of apotheosis by rescuing from divine wrath the very man who was of all men most hateful to Jupiter. Indeed, this rescue is, I think, a myth : one of those many exploits which have been vaguely attributed to Hercules, as are conquests to Don Juan and *mots* to Sheridan. That Prometheus was still Vinctus in the days of Sulla, I shall anon suggest. That he is Vinctus to this day — and none, not even Professor Thorsby, denies that Mr. Mitchell has made out a good *prima facie* case to that effect — is a most surprising and shocking matter for our reflection. Since the middle ages, many philosophers have dwelt on the possibility that the gods of Greece and Rome are not dead. From time to time strange tales have come to us, as that Vulcan was a smith in Verona, Venus was a courtesan in Cyprus itself, and some one suspiciously like Apollo had been seen herding sheep in Picardy. But since Prometheus has been seen in durance on Mount Caucasus it would seem that the gods, so far from trailing a menial existence on this earth, are actually still potent in Olympus. It is not my intention to foreshadow here the wide-reaching influence which Mr. Mitchell's discovery is bound to exercise on the future of mankind. Modern faith and modern thought will have to adapt themselves to the new conditions. Already the bishops and the savants are in a flutter, and the librarian of the Athenæum tells me that the demand for *Lemprière* is quite unprecedented. But what most immediately concerns and moves me is the knowledge that a man is still suffering daily torture for an offence committed in the earliest age of the world's history, for an offence of which, moreover, he may not even have been guilty. At Rome, Demetrius Apollophanes, the sophist whom Sulla brought over from Samothrace, wrote a long treatise to show that Prometheus could not possibly have stolen fire from Olympus, that his trial had been, in fact, arbitrary, vindictive, and farcical, and that he ought to be released forthwith. For this treatise, which raised a storm of popular indignation, Demetrius was arraigned *de impietate in deos*. His friends out of Court sought to prove that the real thief had been, not Prometheus, but Mercury, Jupiter's spy and pander, who had stolen the fire either to gratify a whim of Dryope, or else, as some preferred to think, merely from that naughty impulse which had made him rob Mars of his sword, Apollo of his arrows, and Venus of her girdle. It was further alleged that Jupiter, unwilling to punish a valuable servant who knew much to his discredit, had fastened on Prometheus as a kind of scape-goat. However, when the Sophist appeared in the Forum to stand his trial, public feeling was all for the prosecution. Every one felt that the honour of Olympus would be compromised by an acquittal. The judges declared that the Prometheus affair was *res judicata,* and the defendant's advocate was strictly forbidden even to mention it, though the priests of Jupiter and the priests of Mercury all came down to the Court and swore that Prometheus was guilty, and Demetrius now and again swore by all his literary works — which are not, I believe, extant — that Prometheus was innocent. The whole trial, indeed (if we can trust the fragments of Eutropius, which is its only record), seems to have been rather inconclusive. I refer to it merely with a view to showing that the guilt of Prometheus is not such a certainty as it is sometimes thought to be. If Prometheus was wrongly convicted, no miscarriage of justice was ever more hideous to contemplate. If he was convicted rightly, the sentence passed on him was quite unduly severe. If he was indeed guilty, if it is indeed to his light fingers that we mortals owe our possession of fire, ought we not to regard him as one of our greatest benefactors — a man to whose fate we cannot decently

be indifferent? Fire is the element which, in its flight
upward, typifies all that is noblest in man's nature, even
as water is the symbol of man's weakness and incon-
stancy. Fire is the sacred element. Water, which
cleanses, can corrupt also. Fire cleanses. It alone has
power to refine and purge truly. Without it we walk
in darkness and die in cold. And he, the son of Iapetus,
by whom, perhaps, we were made partakers of this Olympian treasure, is still chained to the rock, facing the terror
of an old torment eternally renewed. Every evening, as
the sun is setting, the eagle wheels over Mount Caucasus.
Lower and lower it wheels, while he who is its deathless
prey shivers in his chains, and gazes up to it with terror
in his eyes, and in a faint voice cries out for pity from
those who are always pitiless. The eagle hovers down.
It pauses on spread wings, and Prometheus sees near to
him the staring yellow eyes, the talons, the beak that will
anon be ripping its familiar meal from his torn flesh.

Enough of words! Prometheus must be rescued, and
that without more delay. It is I who shall rescue him.
To leave him in his present position were a disgrace, not
merely to Russia, but to the whole civilised world. These
words have been written amidst the preparations for my
departure. From Paris I shall travel straight through

Europe, and, once my foot is on Mount Caucasus, I shall not rest till I have reached the summit. Mr. Mitchell declares that summit to be inaccessible till mid-summer. I shall find means to reach it now, nevertheless. I shall hail the captive with words of good cheer — χαῖρε, Ἰαπετιονίδη! — and with my gun I shall shoot the eagle as it hovers over him at sunset, and with a file I shall free him of the rusty fetters that bind him to the rock. Dodging any thunderbolts that may be hurled at me, I shall pick up the shot eagle, and shall lead Prometheus gently down the mountain-side. When we reach the inn in the valley, I shall provide him with the tweed suit which I have ordered for him and am taking with me, the fur coat, the dressing-case whose fittings are marked Π. We shall be in London, if all go well, in time for the latter part of the season. I am sure Prometheus will be much lionised. But even if he be not the success that I anticipate, I shall, at least, have done my duty, and the bird of Jupiter, stuffed, under a glass case, will be always an ornament to my study and a pleasant souvenir of my trip.